Women In History Trivia

Compiled by

Cheryl Pryor

Arlington & Amelia

Copyright © 2018 Cheryl Pryor

Arlington & Amelia Publishing

ArlingtonAmeliaPub@cfl.rr.com

All rights reserved. No portion of this book may be reproduced or transmitted in any form or by any means, electronic or mechanical, including photocopy, recording, or any information storage and retrieval system without permission of the author.

ISBN-10: 1886541388
ISBN-13: 978-1886541382

TABLE OF CONTENTS

1	The Royals	1
2	Women Of Faith	46
3	Women Pirates	56
4	Women of Early American History	63
5	Women of American Revolution	80
6	American Civil Rights Activists	94
7	They Did It First	103
8	Femme Fatales & Badass Women	111
9	Famous Women Authors	120
10	Famous Women Artists	129
11	Outstanding Achievements	138
12	Women Athletes	151
13	Women In Music	159
14	Actresses From Days Ago	174
15	Women of Modern American History	188

About This Book

'Women In History Trivia' *is* a trivia and history book all in one. There are over 500 trivia questions with multiple choice answers. Included are over 300 women who have made history – *the good and the bad.*

You will find included women of royalty from princesses, queens who ruled the land, women pharaohs, czarinas, and empresses.

Women who ruled the high seas as pirates, notorious gangsters, and women of great accomplishments with science, medicine, in flight and space, women who made great discoveries and set historical records.

The arts which includes artists, musicians, and actresses along with fascinating stories of their lives are all included.

The answers are found at the end of each chapter. The page number of the answer key can be found given at the beginning of each chapter. This way you can test yourself without the answer being visible while you are pondering the answer.

You will find throughout the book (under the answer section) interesting tidbits of information given when you see the * symbol.

Some of the women you may recognize immediately, while you may find some you've never heard of that are equally fascinating that will leave you wondering why they were ever left out of history books.

Remember, these are *'women of history,'* so you may find some, but not find many women who are currently in the headlines. They will have to wait their turn until their history is written.

You may find that some of these women may have had what many consider common lives until they felt an interest or passion about a subject that made them act in the way they did, many putting their lives at risk to make a stand for their beliefs. But undoubtedly, you will see why all these women deserve their own place in history.

Other Books by Cheryl Pryor

Where In The U.S. Am I?

Where In The World Am I?

The Big Book of Old Testament Bible Trivia

The Big Book of New Testament Bible Trivia

Living The Word of God

The Big Book of Presidential Trivia

The Big Book of First Ladies Trivia

Presidents, First Ladies, & First Family Trivia

Presidents Trivia Challenge

First Family Trivia

Children Of The Presidents

American Revolution & The Birth of A Nation Trivia

Chosen

Pregnancy Journal

Precious Moments

Treasured Moments of My Child

My Mother's Life Story

My Father's Life Story

How Much Do You *Really* Know About The Love Of Your Life?

Couples Game Night Challenge

RV Travel & Expense Journal

Wedding Survival Guide

Write Now

Legacy

Children's Books

My Child's Keepsake Journal

Trivia For Kids: The Presidents

Trivia For Kids: First Ladies

From the series: The Sullivan Family Series

Savannah In The Big Move

Savannah On Stage

Savannah On Horseback

Savannah in Look What Followed Me Home

Savannah & The Grumpy Neighbor

Savannah & The Mad Scientist

From the series: Savannah's World Travels Series

Savannah's Disney World Celebration

Savannah Goes To Paris

1

THE ROYALS

Queens, Empress, Tsarina, & Women Pharaohs

Answers for this chapter on page 37

1. Under her rule, and that of her husband who ruled jointly, was the beginning of an overseas empire in the New World led by Christopher Columbus under what queen's sponsorship.

    A. Victoria   B. Isabella

    C. Anne   D. Catherine of Aragon

2. This queen was unseated after only 9 days on the throne.

    A. Mary I (Tudor)   B. Liliuokalani

    C. Mary Queen of Scots   D. Lady Jane Grey

3. Who holds the title of longest-reigning monarch in British history?

    A. Victoria   B. Elizabeth I

    C. Elizabeth II   D. Catherine the Great

4. She was Queen of England during the Industrial Revolution.

   A. Victoria   B. Isabella

   C. Anne   D. Catherine de Medici

5. The woman who was Russia's longest-ruling female leader of Russia wasn't even Russian.

   A. Alexandra (Romanov)   B. Cixi

   C. Anne   D. Catherine the Great

6. She was the Queen of France during the French Revolution.

   A. Marie Antoinette   B. Josephine (Bonaparte)

   C. Alexandra   D. Catherine de Medici

7. Which Egyptian queen was known to be the lover of Julius Caesar and of Mark Antony?

   A. Diana   B. Cleopatra

   C. Nefertiti   D. Hatshepsut

8. At her execution her eyes were covered with a cloth. She laid her neck upon the block, commended herself to God, and received the death-stroke. The executioner's hand was unsteady and the first blow merely cut the back of her head. She whispered, "Sweet Jesus," and the executioner struck again a second time. This time with the death blow.

A. Mary I						B. Isabella

C. Mary Queen of Scots		D. Marie Antoinette

9. She was consort of Russian Czar Nicholas II. She along with her entire family were murdered in 1918.

A. Catherine the Great			B. Josephine (Bonaparte)

C. Anne							D. Alexandra

10. Few people in history have been vilified as she has been, the last Empress of China.

A. Victoria						B. Cixi

C. Hatshepsut					D. Liliuokalani

11. Currently located at a museum in Berlin, the bust of this queen is one of the most iconic symbols of Egypt.

A. Cleopatra					B. Nefertiti

C. Hatshepsut					D. Cixi

12. This future queen was not yet three years old when her father had her mother beheaded.

A. Elizabeth I					B. Marie Antoinette

C. Eleanor of Aquitaine			D. Josephine Bonaparte

13. She was the most powerful woman in 12th century Europe.

    A. Eleanor of Aquitaine   B. Isabella

    C. Victoria   D. Catherine the Great

14. Which two queens of Egypt tombs have never been discovered?

    A. Cixi   B. Hatshepsut

    C. Cleopatra   D. Nefertiti

15. She had been one of the Xianfeng Emperor's low-ranking concubines, but her power was in bearing his only son.

    A. Catherine of Aragon   B. Hatshepsut

    C. Cixi   D. Cleopatra

16. She was the first Empress of France.

    A. Marie Antoinette   B. Josephine

    C. Lady Jane Grey   D. Eleanor of Aquitaine

17. In the 15th century B.C., what female pharaoh ruled Egypt in the guise of a man?

    A. Cleopatra   B. Catherine de Medici

    C. Nefertiti   D. Hatshepsut

18. She was the first and the last woman to rule Hawaii.

    A. Elizabeth I   B. Anne

    C. Liliuokalani   D. Isabella

19. She was the queen consort of both King Louis VII of France and King Henry II of England, mother of King Richard I (the Lionheart) and King John (also known as John Lackland) of England.

    A. Catherine de Medici   B. Eleanor of Aquitaine

    C. Mary Queen of Scots   D. Catherine of Aragon

20. It is believed throughout history that she committed suicide by means of an asp, but it has been unproven as to how it occurred.

    A. Cixi   B. Lady Jane Grey

    C. Nefertiti   D. Cleopatra

21. She was one of the most fascinating and controversial monarchs of the 16th century. At one time she claimed the crowns of four nations – Scotland, France, England, and Ireland.

    A. Mary Queen of Scots   B. Elizabeth I

    C. Eleanor of Aquitaine   D. Victoria

22. She was perhaps one of the most powerful women to have ever ruled in ancient Egypt. She saw the wealthiest time in Ancient

Egyptian history.

    A. Hatshepsut   B. Victoria

    C. Nefertiti   D. Cleopatra

23. She was the first wife of King Henry VIII, though he wasn't her first husband. She had previously been married to his older brother.

    A. Mary I   B. Isabella

    C. Lady Jane Grey   D. Catherine of Aragon

24. Her husband abdicated in 1917 as a result of the Russian Revolution.

    A. Josephine   B. Alexandra

    C. Catherine de Medici   D. Catherine the Great

25. She was in large part responsible for the unrest that led to the French Revolution and overthrow of the monarchy.

    A. Josephine   B. Alexandra

    C. Marie Antoinette   D. Catherine of Aragon

26. She was the longest reigning female pharaoh in Egypt.

    A. Hatshepsut   B. Cleopatra

    C. Victoria   D. Nefertiti

27. She was one of the most influential personalities of the Catholic-Huguenot wars.

    A. Catherine de Medici   B. Eleanor of Aquitaine

    C. Anne   D. Catherine of Aragon

28. The first four years of her reign were occupied with the Castilian civil war.

    A. Mary I   B. Elizabeth I

    C. Victoria   D. Isabella

29. During her reign she defeated the Spanish Armada and maintained peace in her previously divided country.

    A. Josephine   B. Elizabeth I

    C. Marie Antoinette   D. Catherine of Aragon

30. She was 18 years of age when she became Queen of England.

    A. Elizabeth I   B. Alexandra

    C. Victoria   D. Elizabeth II

31. Egypt's Alexandria-based rulers or pharaoh's, including which queen of Greek descent, descended from Alexander the Great's general Ptolemy I Soter?

A. Cleopatra   B. Nefertiti

C. Josephine   D. Hatshepsut

32. While Scotland was being ruled by regents in her stead, she spent her childhood in France. In 1558, she married the Dauphin of France and when he ascended to the French throne in 1559 she became queen consort of France. When he died in 1560, she returned to Scotland.

A. Elizabeth I   B. Mary Queen of Scots

C. Victoria   D. Lady Jane Grey

33. She ruled alongside her husband, Pharaoh Akhenaten, during the mid-1300's B.C.

A. Hatshepsut   B. Cleopatra

C. Nefertiti   D. Cixi

34. Under her rule Russia became one of the great powers of Europe.

A. Josephine   B. Catherine de Medici

C. Alexandra   D. Catherine the Great

35. From 1147 to 1149, she accompanied her husband on the Second Crusade. During the Crusades she dressed in armor carrying lances riding a white horse.

A. Catherine de Medici   B. Eleanor of Aquitaine

C. Catherine the Great   D. Catherine of Aragon

36. When the workers and peasants of France took up arms, the royal family in a plot hatched by what queen, attempted to escape the country but were captured?

A. Josephine   B. Alexandra

C. Marie Antoinette   D. Catherine of Aragon

37. **True or False.** Never before Queen Mary I did a woman ever attempt to rule England.

38. After the death of what queen, ended the reign of the house of Tudor?

A. Victoria   B. Anne

C. Elizabeth I   D. Eleanor of Aquitaine

39. Married at age fourteen, she became queen at the age of nineteen.

A. Elizabeth I   B. Marie Antoinette

C. Victoria   D. Catherine the Great

40. Her grandmother Queen Victoria had intended for her to be

Britain's future queen, instead she became the Tsarina of Russia.

    A. Elizabeth I   B. Alexandra

    C. Elizabeth II   D. Anne

41. Her coronation as queen was the first to be televised.

    A. Anne   B. Alexandra

    C. Catherine de Medici   D. Elizabeth II

42. She was considered a catch, a seductress that was intelligent and power-hungry (with a mouthful of black, rotten teeth) that used her feminine charms to interest a 26-year old general who would later become emperor of France.

    A. Josephine   B. Catherine the Great

    C. Catherine de Medici   D. Catherine of Aragon

43. She came to power in a bloodless coup that later turned deadly.

    A. Josephine   B. Catherine the Great

    C. Victoria   D. Catherine of Aragon

44. Before becoming Queen of France, she was Archduchess of Austria and was the daughter of Habsburg Empress Maria Theresa and Francis I, Holy Roman Emperor.

    A. Eleanor of Aquitaine   B. Victoria

    C. Catherine of Aragon   D. Marie Antoinette

45. One of her daughters was Catherine of Aragon, Henry VIII's first wife.

    A. Eleanor of Aquitaine   B. Isabella

    C. Victoria   D. Mary I

46. She was described as "a queen who surpassed almost all the queens of the world."

    A. Eleanor of Aquitaine   B. Victoria

    C. Marie Antoinette   D. Alexandra

47. She was the first wife of Napoleon Bonaparte.

    A. Anne   B. Eleanor of Aquitaine

    C. Josephine   D. Catherine de Medici

48. **True or False.** As a constitutional monarch, Queen Elizabeth II does not weigh in on political matters or voice her political opinion, but she does meet with her prime ministers and is kept abreast of matters.

49. She was buried in splendor draped in diamonds, but in later

years her tomb was raided.

    A. Cixi   B. Cleopatra

    C. Alexandra   D. Marie Antoinette

50. Two of her daughters became queens of Egypt.

    A. Nefertiti   B. Victoria

    C. Cleopatra   D. Liliuokalani

51. She was born a princess of Spain in 1485 (her parents were Queen Isabella and King Ferdinand) and later became Queen of England in 1509 (she was the first wife of Henry VIII).

    A. Eleanor of Aquitaine   B. Catherine of Aragon

    C. Isabella   D. Mary I

52. These two half-sisters, both queens, are buried in the same tomb in London's Westminster Abbey.

    A. Elizabeth I   B. Catherine of Aragon

    C. Isabella   D. Mary I

53. She gave birth to ten children. Two were of French royalty and eight of them were of British royalty. (*How did she manage that?)

    A. Victoria   B. Catherine of Aragon

    C. Isabella   D. Eleanor of Aquitaine

54. Her sister Mary I, queen before her, worked to restore England to Roman Catholicism; but when this queen took the throne during her first session in Parliament, she called for the passage of the Act of Supremacy re-establishing the Church of England.

    A. Mary Queen of Scots   B. Victoria

    C. Elizabeth I   D. Elizabeth II

55. During her son's reign an attempt was made to remove all traces of her as a ruler, even to the point of having her monuments torn down and her name removed from the official king list.

    A. Eleanor of Aquitaine   B. Hatshepsut

    C. Anne   D. Mary Queen of Scots

56. She became famous when she married the heir to the English throne and even more famous when she divorced him. Her sudden dramatic death at an early age made her even more beloved by the people.

    A. Alexandra   B. Catherine of Aragon

    C. Marie Antoinette   D. Diana Wales

57. The Boxer Rebellion took place while she was Empress of China.

    A. Josephine   B. Anne

    C. Liliuokalani   D. Cixi

58. At the time she inherited the throne of England, the country was at war with France.

    A. Mary I   B. Elizabeth I

    C. Mary Queen of Scots   D. Anne

59. She was Queen of Egypt during the 1st century B.C. and is one of the most famous female rulers in history.

    A. Cleopatra   B. Nefertiti

    C. Hatshepsut   D. Cixi

60. She, along with her husband King Ferdinand, are responsible for the unification of Spain.

    A. Eleanor of Aquitaine   B. Catherine of Aragon

    C. Isabella   D. Mary I

61. Born in Germany she was the last Empress of the Russian Empire.

    A. Victoria   B. Catherine of Aragon

    C. Catherine the Great   D. Alexandra

62. At one point she was arrested and sent to the Tower of London by her older sister and narrowly escaped her mother's fate of beheading before she herself became queen.

A. Marie Antoinette   B. Elizabeth I

C. Lady Jane Grey   D. Mary I

63. Her disappearance from historical records and her demise remain a mystery. Perhaps some questions will be answered if her tomb is ever found. Until then, she remains Egypt's mysterious queen.

     A. Cleopatra   B. Cixi

     C. Nefertiti   D. Hatshepsut

64. She had her own sister imprisoned at the Tower of London.

     A. Mary I   B. Elizabeth I

     C. Mary Queen of Scots   D. Lady Jane Gray

65. Beginning in 1478 B.C. she reigned in Egypt for over twenty years alongside of her husband Thutmose II, and after his death as co-regent with her step-son.

     A. Nefertiti   B. Cleopatra

     C. Hatshepsut   D. Victoria

66. John Dudley, Earl of Warwick, plotted into how he would make her queen, so in turn his own son would become king. However, once she was crowned she refused to name her husband as king claiming he had no right to possess the title but instead

stated he would become a duke. It really didn't matter as a short time later they were both imprisoned, tried for treason, and executed. Who was she?

    A. Mary Queen of Scots   B. Anne

    C. Elizabeth I   D. Lady Jane Grey

67. This queen had her own private castle on the grounds of the Palace of Versailles.

    A. Eleanor of Aquitaine   B. Josephine

    C. Marie Antoinette   D. Catherine de Medici

68. At the end of her reign Russia had expanded westward and southward over an area of more than 200,000 square miles, built an additional 100 new towns, trade expanded, along with military victories. These achievements have won her a distinguished place in history.

    A. Victoria   B. Catherine the Great

    C. Alexandra   D. Josephine

69. She gave birth in 1904 to a son, the future heir they had longed for after four daughters. It was soon discovered he suffered from hemophilia.

    A. Victoria   B. Catherine the Great

    C. Josephine   D. Alexandra

70. She was the last queen of the Macedonian dynasty that ruled Egypt between the death of Alexander the Great and it's annexation by Rome.

    A. Nefertiti   B. Josephine

    C. Cleopatra   D. Victoria

71. After the death of her son she adopted her three year old nephew and had him named the new heir, while she continued to act as regent.

    A. Cixi   B. Catherine of Aragon

    C. Catherine de Medici   D. Elizabeth I

72. In the diary of Leon Trotsky it was revealed that the assassinations of what empress along with her entire family were personally ordered to be carried out by Lenin?

    A. Catherine the Great   B. Anne

    C. Alexandra   D. Marie Antoinette

73. Her father King James V, King of Scotland, died when she was only six days old and she acceded to the throne.

    A. Eleanor of Aquitaine   B. Mary Queen of Scots

    C. Isabella   D. Anne

74. Due to her marriage to her first husband, her life was

endangered during the French Revolution when her first husband was guillotined for the role he had in the Revolutionary army. She herself was imprisoned for a time and even scheduled for execution, but with the aid of high-placed friends was set free. She lived to one day become empress.

    A. Josephine   B. Marie Antoinette

    C. Isabella   D. Catherine of Aragon

75. The refusal of Pope Clement VII to annul this queen's marriage to the king is what led to the English Reformation.

    A. Eleanor of Aquitaine   B. Mary I

    C. Victoria   D. Catherine of Aragon

76. In 1913, a team led by German archaeologist Ludwig Borchardt discovered a sculpture buried upside down in the excavated workshop of royal sculptor Thutmose. With an agreement to split any artifacts found with the Egyptian government the item was kept as part of Germany's portion. It was given to Jacques Simon who had funded the expedition who displayed it at his home for the next eleven years. The bust later came into the hands of Hitler who treasured the bust. Hitler refused to return it to Egypt. It was hidden in a salt mine throughout WWII to keep it safe. Today it is one of the most recognizable icons of Egypt and viewed by over 500,000 visitors a year. Who is the sculpture of?

    A. Cleopatra   B. Cixi

    C. Nefertiti   D. Hatshepsut

77. She was only the third woman to become pharaoh in 3,000 years of Ancient Egyptian history and was the first to attain full power.

    A. Hatshepsut   B. Cleopatra

    C. Josephine   D. Nefertiti

78. A U.S. military-backed coup removed this queen from power. She signed a formal abdication but continued to appeal to the U.S. president for reinstatement.

    A. Alexandra   B. Liliuokalani

    C. Anne   D. Josephine

79. Her life was a threat to the throne of Queen Elizabeth I. Elizabeth feared the Catholics would plot to put her on the English throne in place of her. Some did indeed feel she had more right to the throne than the queen herself who many considered to be illegitimate.

    A. Mary Queen of Scots   B. Catherine of Aragon

    C. Anne   D. Mary I

80. She is remembered for the elaborate wigs she wore in a hairstyle she made famous called the pouf. The wigs were decorated with feathers and jewels and often had a theme to them.

    A. Josephine   B. Cixi

    C. Maria Antoinette   D. Catherine de Medici

81. One of her daughters was King Tut's queen.

   A. Cleopatra   B. Nefertiti

   C. Victoria   D. Hatshepsut

82. Not only was she the Queen of the United Kingdom and Ireland, but she was also Empress of India.

   A. Elizabeth II   B. Elizabeth I

   C. Victoria   D. Mary I

83. Her inability to give her husband a son put a strain on their marriage and became the reason he had their marriage annulled and married a second time to the daughter of Emperor Francis I of Austria.

   A. Catherine of Aragon   B. Josephine

   C. Isabella   D. Catherine the Great

84. Born into British nobility, she became a member of the British royal family as the first wife of Charles, Prince of Wales, the heir apparent to the British throne. She was the mother of Prince William, Duke of Cambridge who is second in line to the throne.

   A. Elizabeth I   B. Catherine of Aragon

   C. Diana Wales   D. Sophie Wessex

85. *True or False.* The Elizabethan Era was named for Queen

Elizabeth II.

86. She was the first queen and last monarch of the Kingdom of Hawaii, ruling from 1891 till 1893.

    A. Eleanor of Aquitaine   B. Cixi

    C. Liliuokalani   D. Anne

87. She became Britain's first queen since Queen Victoria in 1901.

    A. Elizabeth I   B. Mary I

    C. Anne   D. Elizabeth II

88. She attained unprecedented power for a woman and took on the full titles and regalia of a pharaoh.

    A. Cleopatra   B. Hatshepsut

    C. Cixi   D. Nefertiti

89. Which queen actively persecuted Protestants and burned offenders at the stake?

    A. Eleanor of Aquitaine   B. Catherine of Aragon

    C. Mary I   D. Mary Queen of Scots

90. The last Stuart monarch, she was Queen of Great Britain and Ireland from 1702 till 1714.

A. Anne   B. Eleanor of Aquitaine

C. Elizabeth I   D. Victoria

91. At thirty-seven years of age she was beheaded by the guillotine.

   A. Mary I   B. Catherine of Aragon

   C. Marie Antoinette   D. Lady Jane Grey

92. As queen she attempted to return England from Protestantism to Roman Catholicism, and in this attempt she had three hundred religious dissenters executed including the Archbishop of Canterbury.

   A. Mary I   B. Elizabeth I

   C. Mary Queen of Scots   D. Anne

93. Parents on both sides disapproved of this marital match. On her husband's side the disapproval came in large part because it was suspected (and later proven a valid point) that she was a carrier of the hereditary disease of hemophilia. Their only son and heir would indeed be born with the disease. Who was she?

   A. Victoria   B. Alexandra

   C. Elizabeth II   D. Lady Jane Grey

94. She was Empress Dowager of China.

A. Victoria   B. Cixi

C. Josephine   D. Alexandra

95. What queen had nine children; one of which would become King of Great Britain and the others all married into the royal families of Germany, Sweden, Romania, Russia, and Denmark?

     A. Eleanor of Aquitaine   B. Mary Queen of Scots

     C. Isabella   D. Victoria

96. She was the first married queen to rule England.

     A. Eleanor of Aquitaine   B. Mary I

     C. Anne   D. Victoria

97. She is one of the most compelling and tragic figures in Tudor history. She was forced against her will to become queen, a title she held for only nine days and afterward was beheaded.

     A. Lady Jane Grey   B. Catherine of Aragon

     C. Mary Queen of Scots   D. Mary I

98. Fears of an assassination against what queen increased after Pope Gregory XIII proclaimed in 1580 that it would be no sin to rid the world of such a miserable heretic?

A. Mary I   B. Catherine of Aragon

C. Mary Queen of Scots   D. Elizabeth I

99. She was an Italian noblewoman who was Queen of France from 1547 until 1559 by her marriage to King Henry II.

A. Eleanor of Aquitaine   B. Catherine de Medici

C. Isabella   D. Josephine

100. What Egyptian queen's actions influenced the formation of the Roman Empire?

A. Cleopatra   B. Nefertiti

C. Josephine   D. Hatshepsut

101. Queen Elizabeth I had this queen imprisoned for nineteen years and eventually beheaded, but upon Queen Elizabeth's death, this queen's son became king of England as King James I.

A. Mary I   B. Catherine of Aragon

C. Lady Jane Grey   D. Mary Queen of Scots

102. On the walls of tombs and temples she is depicted alongside her husband with a frequency shown for no other Egyptian queen. Many of these depictions show her in a position of power and authority.

| A. Hatshepsut | B. Cixi |
| C. Nefertiti | D. Cleopatra |

103. At the death of her husband the prince, what British monarch slept with a plaster cast of his hand by her side and went into seclusion for twenty-five years forever after wearing only black?

| A. Eleanor of Aquitaine | B. Victoria |
| C. Anne | D. Mary I |

104. Her association with mystic and "faith healer" Rasputin brought on the wrath of the Russian people.

| A. Elizabeth I | B. Alexandra |
| C. Catherine de Medici | D. Catherine the Great |

105. She was Queen of France from 1547 until 1559 and the mother of Kings Francis II, Charles IX, and Henry III. From 1560 till 1563, she ruled France as regent for her son Charles IX, King of France.

| A. Eleanor of Aquitaine | B. Marie Antoinette |
| C. Catherine de Medici | D. Mary Queen of Scots |

106. Queen Elizabeth II is from the House of _____.

| A. Tudor | B. York |
| C. Lancaster | D. Windsor |

107. What two Queens of England celebrated their Diamond Jubilees (60 years on the throne)?

    A. Victoria

    B. Elizabeth I

    C. Elizabeth II

    D. Eleanor of Aquitaine

108. She was the mother of "the lost Dauphin."

    A. Eleanor of Aquitaine

    B. Josephine

    C. Marie Antoinette

    D. Mary Queen of Scots

109. After her death two year-old Pu Yi became China's last Emperor.

    A. Liliuokalani

    B. Cixi

    C. Josephine

    D. Catherine de Medici

110. During her years as monarch Britain expanded it's imperial reach; doubling in size by adding Australia, India, Canada, and other areas.

    A. Eleanor of Aquitaine

    B. Elizabeth I

    C. Anne

    D. Victoria

111. She is considered one of Egypt's most successful pharaohs.

    A. Cleopatra

    B. Cixi

    C. Hatshepsut

    D. Nefertiti

112. As with many royals, she and her husband were related to each other via several lines of European royalty. The most notable being was a great-grandmother they shared who was the Princess Wilhelmine of Baden. Her husband's paternal grandmother, Empress Maria Alexandrovna, was her paternal aunt. Her great-great grandfather King Frederick William II of Prussia was her husband's great-great-great grandfather. Who was she?

    A. Alexandra   B. Victoria

    C. Isabella   D. Elizabeth II

113. She was the daughter of King Ferdinand and Queen Isabella, rulers of Spain most remembered to the world as the backers of Christopher Columbus' voyages. She was betrothed to the son and heir of King Henry VII of England.

    A. Eleanor of Aquitaine   B. Catherine of Aragon

    C. Mary I   D. Catherine de Medici

114. She and her husband established the cult of Aten, the sun god.

    A. Elizabeth II   B. Hatshepsut

    C. Nefertiti   D. Cixi

115. Inheriting a vast estate at the age of fifteen she was one of the most sought after brides of her generation. She became one of the most powerful and influential figures of the Middle Ages.

A. Eleanor of Aquitaine   B. Catherine of Aragon

C. Isabella   D. Marie Antoinette

116. She was Empress of Russia in the late 1700's.

   A. Alexandra   B. Josephine

   C. Isabella   D. Catherine the Great

117. Queen for the shortest time of any royal in England's history, she remains one of the most famous Queens of England – more for her history than of any accomplishments.

   A. Anne   B. Lady Jane Grey

   C. Mary I   D. Josephine

118. A skilled musician, this queen wrote more than 160 songs.

   A. Liliuokalani   B. Catherine of Aragon

   C. Elizabeth I   D. Marie Antoinette

119. In 1792 the National Convention abolished the monarchy, declared the establishment of a French Republic and arrested the king and queen. Who was Queen of France at this time?

   A. Eleanor of Aquitaine   B. Mary Queen of Scots

   C. Marie Antoinette   D. Josephine

120. What queen, unwilling to share power, remained unmarried throughout her lifetime?

    A. Anne

    B. Elizabeth I

    C. Lady Jane Grey

    D. Mary I

121. She was the last active ruler of the Ptolemaic Kingdom of Egypt, after which Egypt became a province of the Roman Empire.

    A. Cleopatra

    B. Victoria

    C. Nefertiti

    D. Hatshepsut

122. This queen helped to negotiate the Act of Union in which England and Scotland were ruled as Great Britain.

    A. Eleanor of Aquitaine

    B. Catherine of Aragon

    C. Mary Queen of Scots

    D. Anne

123. Her grandfather was King George III who was king when England lost it's American colonies.

    A. Josephine

    B. Catherine of Aragon

    C. Victoria

    D. Eleanor of Aquitaine

124. She is the only British monarch to ever celebrate her Sapphire Jubilee, which is 65 years on the throne.

A. Eleanor of Aquitaine		B. Elizabeth II

C. Elizabeth I		D. Victoria

125. At birth she was 5th in line to the throne. No one suspected she would one day sit on the throne.

A. Victoria		B. Marie Antoinette

C. Isabella		D. Elizabeth II

126. She was the last sovereign of the Kamehameha dynasty which had ruled since 1810.

A. Eleanor of Aquitaine		B. Catherine the Great

C. Liliuokalani		D. Alexandra

127. Held prisoner she was forced to sign a document abdicating the throne in favor of her year-old son.

A. Mary Queen of Scots		B. Catherine of Aragon

C. Liliuokalani		D. Mary I

128. What Egyptian Queen was King Tut's (Tutankhamun) stepmother?

A. Hatshepsut		B. Cleopatra

C. Victoria		D. Nefertiti

129. Her greatest achievement during her reign was the building of the memorial temple at Deir-el-Bahari, considered one of the architectural wonders of Ancient Egypt.

    A. Cleopatra   B. Hatshepsut

    C. Victoria   D. Nefertiti

130. While her husband was off to the front during WWI she served as regent, though she was largely unpopular to the people she ruled.

    A. Alexandra   B. Liliuokalani

    C. Isabella   D. Eleanor of Aquitaine

131. Not counting the nine day queen who was considered a de facto queen, she was England's first female monarch.

    A. Mary Queen of Scots   B. Lady Jane Grey

    C. Mary I   D. Victoria

132. She was queen to France's King Louis XVI.

    A. Mary Queen of Scots   B. Marie Antoinette

    C. Josephine   D. Isabella

133. During her reign she built and restored monuments, one of which was a pair of red granite obelisks at the Temple of Amon at Karnak, one of which still stands today.

A. Hatshepsut   B. Cleopatra

C. Cixi   D. Nefertiti

134. When invited to Russia to meet the heir to the throne as a potential bride, she later wrote that she was more attracted to the crown of Russia which the heir would one day wear, than she was to the heir himself.

A. Mary Queen of Scots   B. Catherine the Great

C. Alexandra   D. Victoria

135. At age fifteen she was her father's heir to an estate larger than that even of the King of France. At her father's death she inherited his title and lands and was placed under the guardianship of the King of France. Within hours she became betrothed to the king's son and heir.

A. Mary Queen of Scots   B. Marie Antoinette

C. Isabella   D. Eleanor of Aquitaine

136. **True or False.** Cleopatra married her ten year old brother after their father's death.

137. Married a short time before her sixteenth birthday to the heir of the English throne, she became a widow less than six months later. When her second husband later wished to invalidate their marriage or have it annulled, as he said, 'it was unlawful for him to have married his brother's wife' (which actually had nothing to do

with his true reason; he wished for a son which she was unable to produce and he already had his next bride-to-be waiting). She swore on the sacrament to a papal legate that her first marriage was never consummated.

    A. Catherine of Aragon   B. Elizabeth I

    C. Eleanor of Aquitaine   D. Anne

138. Shortly before her death, having no heirs she named James VI of Scotland as her successor.

    A. Mary Queen of Scots   B. Elizabeth I

    C. Anne   D. Mary I

139. She is said to have had a son with Julius Caesar and twins with Mark Antony.

    A. Catherine de Medici   B. Eleanor of Aquitaine

    C. Nefertiti   D. Cleopatra

140. How is Queen Elizabeth II related to Queen Victoria?

    A. They aren't related in any way   B. On her husband's side of the family

    C. Great-great granddaughter   D. Cousins many times removed

141. With the conclusion of the Seven Years War in 1763, in order to preserve a fragile alliance between Austria and France typical of the times, she was used to cement alliances by marrying the

grandson and heir to the French monarch.

    A. Mary Antoinette   B. Catherine of Aragon

    C. Eleanor of Aquitaine   D. Mary Queen of Scots

142. When she became lover of Caesar and Roman reinforcements arrived, her brother lost his hold on the throne, fled, and drowned in the Nile.

    A. Hatshepsut   B. Nefertiti

    C. Liliuokalani   D. Cleopatra

143. Of the Manchu Yehenara clan, this Chinese empress dowager and regent controlled the Chinese government in the late Qing dynasty for forty-seven years, from 1861 till her death in 1908.

    A. Victoria   B. Cixi

    C. Liliuokalani   D. Elizabeth I

144. She was Russia's longest-ruling female leader.

    A. Josephine   B. Alexandra

    C. Catherine the Great   D. Liliuokalani

145. She, along with her husband, organized the Spanish Inquisition.

A. Isabella   B. Catherine of Aragon

C. Catherine de Medici   D. Mary I

146. Which two queens are the two longest-serving monarchs in British history?

   A. Eleanor of Aquitaine   B. Victoria

   C. Elizabeth I   D. Elizabeth II

147. She is given credit for teaching the French how to eat with a fork.

   A. Catherine de Medici   B. Mary Queen of Scots

   C. Josephine   D. Marie Antoinette

148. Her life was much like a modern day soap opera: married to two kings, suffering infidelities from both of them, played a part in a revolt against her husband, was captured, sought refugee with her first husband, imprisoned, administered the realm in her son's stead during his crusade to the Holy Land, collected a ransom when her son was taken prisoner and went herself to free her son the king from his captors, and thwarted an attempt to take over power by another son.

   A. Mary Queen of Scots   B. Catherine of Aragon

   C. Eleanor of Aquitaine   D. Mary I

149. Which Queen of England was the last of the House of Hanover?

    A. Mary I   B. Victoria

    C. Anne   D. Eleanor of Aquitaine

150. In 1903, archaeologist Howard Carter discovered her sarcophagus (one of three she prepared), but it was empty. In 2007, archaeologists discovered her mummy which now lies in the Egyptian Museum in Cairo.

    A. Hatshepsut   B. Nefertiti

    C. Cixi   D. Cleopatra

Answers - Chapter 1 - The Royals

1. B - Isabella

2. D - Lady Jane Grey

3. C - Elizabeth II

4. A - Victoria

5. D - Catherine the Great

*She was the daughter of a Prussian Prince. Her birth name wasn't Catherine, it was Sophie von Anhalt-Zerbst. Once she was "approved" as a bride for the sitting empresses' heir Peter (the empress at the time was the daughter of Peter the Great), her name was changed to Yekaterina or Catherine and she converted to the Russian Orthodox faith.

6. A - Marie Antoinette

7. B - Cleopatra

8. C - Mary Queen of Scots

9. D - Alexandra (Feodorovna Romanov)

10. B - Cixi (also spelled Tzu Hsi)

11. B - Nefertiti

12. A - Elizabeth I

13. A - Eleanor of Aquitaine

14. C & D - Nefertiti and Cleopatra

15. C - Cixi

16. B - Josephine (Bonaparte)

17. D - Hatshepsut

18. C - Liliuokalani

19. B - Eleanor of Aquitaine

20. D - Cleopatra

21. A - Mary Queen of Scots

22. C - Nefertiti

23. D - Catherine of Aragon

24. B - Alexandra (Romanov)

25. C - Marie Antoinette

26. A - Hatshepsut

27. A - Catherine de Medici

28. D - Isabella

29. B - Elizabeth I

30. C - Victoria

31. A - Cleopatra

32. B - Mary Queen of Scots

33. C - Nefertiti

34. D - Catherine the Great

35. B - Eleanor of Aquitaine

36. C - Marie Antoinette

37. False

*In the 12th century, Matilda tried to take the throne but was ultimately thrown out of the country. Lady Jane Grey reluctantly took the throne for 9 days before Mary I, the rightful heir, came to power.

38. C - Elizabeth I

39. B - Marie Antoinette

40. B - Alexandra

41. D - Elizabeth II

42. A - Josephine

43. B - Catherine the Great

*Just six months after becoming czar, deeply unpopular the military regiment arranged for Peter's arrest. Peter abdicated and Catherine was proclaimed sole ruler. What began as a bloodless coup changed when the brother of Catherine's lover murdered the former czar. It's unknown if Catherine was aware of the plan.

44. D - Marie Antoinette

45. B – Isabella

46. A - Eleanor of Aquitaine

47. C - Josephine

48. True

49. A - Cixi

50. A - Nefertiti

51. B - Catherine of Aragon

52. A & D - Mary I & Elizabeth I

53. D - Eleanor of Aquitaine

* She was first married to a French king and had 2 children with him and later married to the King of England and had 8 children with him.

54. C - Elizabeth I

55. B - Hatshepsut

Hatshepsut's name was forgotten and unknown until 1822 when hieroglyphics were interpreted. Initially the discrepancy of the male-female image confounded the historians; as the time she gained power her images were depicted with a male body – not to pass herself off as a man, but to depict herself as a king in her own right.

56. D – Diana Wales, better known as Princess Di

57. D - Cixi

58. B – Elizabeth I

59. A - Cleopatra

60. C - Isabella

61. D - Alexandra

62. B - Elizabeth I

63. C - Nefertiti

64. A - Mary I (also known as Mary Tudor)

65. C - Hatshepsut

66. D - Lady Jane Grey

67. C - Marie Antoinette

*In addition to the royal palace she also had a rustic retreat on the grounds, Hameau de la Reine (the Queen's Hamlet) with a lake, gardens, and a rustic village where the queen and her friends dressed up as peasants when they tired of palace life. Both places, her private castle and the rustic retreat, can still be visited today at the Palace of Versailles.

68. B - Catherine the Great

69. D - Alexandra

70. C - Cleopatra

71. A - Cixi

72. C - Alexandra

73. B - Mary Queen of Scots

74. A - Josephine

75. D - Catherine of Aragon

The English Reformation led to the break up of the Church of England from the Pope and the Roman Catholic Church.

76. C - Nefertiti

77. A - Hatshepsut

Cleopatra would also assume full power of the position 14 centuries later.

78. B - Liliuokalani

79. A - Mary Queen of Scots

80. C - Marie Antoinette

81. B - Nefertiti

Her name was Ankhesenpaaten and she was not only his queen but his half-sister.

82. C - Victoria

83. B - Josephine

84. C - Diana Wales

85. False

It was named for Elizabeth I

86. C - Liliuokalani

87. D - Elizabeth II

88. B - Hatshepsut

89. C - Mary I

90. A - Anne

91. C - Marie Antoinette

92. A - Mary I

93. B - Alexandra

94. B - Cixi

95. D - Victoria

96. C - Anne

97. A - Lady Jane Grey

98. D - Elizabeth I

99. B - Catherine de Medici

100. A - Cleopatra

101. D - Mary, Queen of Scots

102. C - Nefertiti

103. B - Victoria

104. B - Alexandra

105. C - Catherine de Medici

106. D - Windsor

107. A & C - Victoria & Elizabeth II

108. C - Marie Antoinette

*The title, "the lost Dauphin" came about due to rumors regarding Marie Antoinette's son and the heir to the French throne in regards to his uncertain demise during the Reign of Terror during the French Revolution. There was a rumor that circulated that the boy who actually died was an impostor. Over the years many impostors came forward claiming to be the lost Dauphin and wishing to claim his title. In the year 2000, DNA tests were done by examining the preserved heart of the boy who had died in the prison with samples of hair from his mother Marie Antoinette. It was verified that the boy who died in the prison was indeed the Dauphin.

109. B - Cixi

110. D - Victoria

111. C - Hatshepsut

112. A - Alexandra

113. B - Catherine of Aragon

114. C - Nefertiti

115. A - Eleanor of Aquitaine

116. D - Catherine the Great

117. B - Lady Jane Grey

118. A - Liliuokalani

*She wrote what became the national anthem of Hawaii.

119. C - Marie Antoinette

120. B - Elizabeth I

121. A - Cleopatra

122. D - Anne

123. C - Victoria

124. B - Elizabeth II

125. A - Victoria

126. C - Liliuokalani

127. A - Mary Queen of Scots

128. D - Nefertiti

129. B - Hatshepsut

130. A - Alexandra

131. C - Mary I

132. B - Marie Antoinette

133. A – Hatshepsut

134. B - Catherine the Great

135. D - Eleanor of Aquitaine

136. True

*It is believed to be true though not proven. The throne passed to the two of them though she became the dominant ruler. Later she was forced to flee Egypt and returned with an army and returned to fight her brother/husband for the throne.

137. A - Catherine of Aragon

138. B - Elizabeth I

*James VI, Elizabeth I's successor was son of her former rival to the throne Mary Queen of Scots. It can be a bit confusing but in Scotland he was James VI, but James I in England (due to being the first King of England named James).

139. D - Cleopatra

140. C - Elizabeth II is Queen Victoria's great-great granddaughter.

*Elizabeth II's husband, Prince Philip, Duke of Edinburgh, is a great-great grandson of Queen Victoria.

141. A - Marie Antoinette

142. D - Cleopatra

143. B - Cixi

144. C - Catherine the Great

145. A - Isabella

146. B & D - Victoria and Elizabeth II

*Victoria reigned from 1837 – 1901. Elizabeth II was crowned in 1952 and as of 2018 is still wearing the crown.

147. A - Catherine de Medici

148. C - Eleanor of Aquitaine

149. B - Victoria

150. A - Hatshepsut

2

WOMEN OF FAITH

Answers for this chapter on page 54

1. Who was the first woman mentioned in the Bible?

    A. Mary   B. Esther

    C. Eve   D. Sarah

2. What young, poor Jewish girl was given the most important job in history?

    A. Elizabeth   B. Esther

    C. Miriam   D. Mary

3. She is considered one of the 20th century's greatest humanitarians.

    A. Joan of Arc   B. Mother Teresa

    C. Fanny Crosby   D. Anne Hutchinson

4. Who is a national heroine of France, who led the French army to

a momentous victory during the Hundred Years War?

    A. Mary Magdalene   B. Esther

    C. Joan of Arc   D. Deborah

5. Who was the first person to whom Jesus appeared after his resurrection?

    A. Mary Magdalene   B. Mary

    C. Miriam   D. Ruth

6. She was the sister of Moses who watched from a hiding place nearby when he was placed in a basket and placed in the Nile in order to save his life. The pharaoh had decreed all Hebrew boy babies be put to death. It was the daughter of the pharaoh who found him and raised him as her own. When his sister discovered the princess planned to keep him and not hurt him she bravely stepped forward and arranged with the princess for a Hebrew wet nurse, which was Moses' own mother.

    A. Ruth   B. Esther

    C. Deborah   D. Miriam

7. Who was the peasant girl living in medieval France who believed God had chosen her to lead France to victory in it's war with England?

    A. Deborah   B. Esther

    C. Eve   D. Joan of Arc

8. What was the name of the mother of Jesus?

    A. Esther   *B. Mary*

    C. Eve   *D. Sarah*

9. She was a Jewish queen who has an entire book of the Bible about her.

    A. Elizabeth   *B. Esther*

    C. Deborah   *D. Sarah*

10. What woman of the Bible saved two of Joshua's spies by hiding them and helping them to escape?

    A. Rahab   *B. Ruth*

    C. Deborah   *D. Elizabeth*

11. At the Crucifixion of Jesus, who did Jesus place in the care of John the Apostle?

    A. Mary Magdalene   *B. Ruth*

    C. Mary   *D. Sarah*

12. What woman in the Bible, laughed when she heard that she, a barren woman, was to give birth to a son at the age of ninety?

    A. Eve   *B. Esther*

    C. Ruth   *D. Sarah*

13. Mother of 15 children, what woman's strong religious convictions differed from the Puritans of New England who banished her from their colony?

    A. Mother Teresa   B. Fanny Crosby

    C. Joan of Arc   D. Anne Hutchinson

14. Who was captured, tried for witchcraft, heresy, and burned at the stake at the age of 19?

    A. Esther   B. Joan of Arc

    C. Anne Hutchinson   D. Ruth

15. What poet, lyricist, and composer wrote thousands of Christian songs despite being blind?

    A. Anne Hutchinson   B. Elizabeth

    C. Fanny Crosby   D. Deborah

16. What woman of the Bible was told to tie a cord of scarlet thread and hang it in her window in order to save her life and the lives of her family?

    A. Rahab   B. Deborah

    C. Eve   D. Miriam

17. What woman of the Bible was a prophet and judge of Israel?

    A. Mary Magdalene	B. Deborah

    C. Rahab	D. Elizabeth

18. She received the Nobel Peace Prize for her humanitarian work.

    A. Eve	B. Joan of Arc

    C. Mother Teresa	D. Fanny Crosby

19. There are only two books in the Bible named for women. What two women are these?

    A. Mary	B. Esther

    C. Sarah	D. Ruth

20. During her lifetime she never traveled further than from Nazareth to Egypt, yet her name has endured throughout the ages and reached every corner of the earth.

    A. Eve	B. Joan of Arc

    C. Mary	D. Sarah

21. She was one of the most prolific hymnists in history, writing over 8,000 hymns and gospel songs in her lifetime.

    A. Fanny Crosby	B. Anne Hutchinson

    C. Deborah	D. Sarah

22. She is a heroine of the Jews, as due to her heroic act she saved all the Jews in the Persian empire.

    A. Mary   B. Esther

    C. Miriam   D. Rahab

23. What woman in the Bible was guilty of introducing sin into the world?

    A. Sarah   B. Mary Magdalene

    C. Eve   D. Sarah

24. To what woman in the Bible was this said: "Blessed among women are you, and blessed is the fruit of your womb"?

    A. Elizabeth   B. Esther

    C. Mary   D. Sarah

25. She was the adopted daughter of Mordecai (from the tribe of Benjamin) who saved Mordecai from Haman who plotted to hang him.

    A. Mother Teresa   B. Esther

    C. Ruth   D. Sarah

26. She was awarded the Jewel of India the highest honor bestowed on Indian civilians, as well as the now-defunct Soviet Union's Gold Medal of the Soviet Peace Committee, and the Nobel

Peace Prize in recognition of her work in bringing help to suffering humanity.

    A. Mother Teresa   B. Anne Hutchinson

    C. Joan of Arc   D. Fanny Crosby

27. What woman of the Bible feeling great compassion and love for her mother-in-law after losing both of her sons and her husband stayed with her rather than returning to her own homeland?

    A. Rahab   B. Deborah

    C. Ruth   D. Sarah

28. Religious leader and midwife, what woman in the early 1600's was excommunicated by the Church of Boston and a few years later killed in an Indian raid in New York?

    A. Deborah   B. Anne Hutchinson

    C. Fanny Crosby   D. Sarah

29. The Jewish annual festival Purim, came about to commemorate her courage and the deliverance of the Jews.

    A. Esther   B. Deborah

    C. Eve   D. Sarah

30. She was the mother of John the Baptist and cousin of Mary, mother of Jesus.

Women In History Trivia

A. Mary Magdalene

B. Esther

C. Miriam

D. Elizabeth

Answers - Chapter 2 – Women of Faith

1. C - Eve

2. D - Mary (the mother of Jesus)

*The most important job in the world was to give birth and to raise the son of God.

3. B - Mother Teresa

4. C - Joan of Arc

5. A - Mary Magdalene

6. D - Miriam

7. D - Joan of Arc

8. B - Mary

9. B - Esther

10. A - Rahab

11. C - Mary

12. D - Sarah

13. D - Anne Hutchinson

14. B - Joan of Arc

15. C - Fanny Crosby

16. A - Rahab

17. B - Deborah

18. C - Mother Teresa

19. B & D - Esther & Ruth

20. C - Mary

21. A - Fanny Crosby

22. B - Esther

23. C - Eve

24. C - Mary

25. B - Esther

26. A - Mother Teresa

27. C - Ruth

28. B - Anne Hutchinson

29. A - Esther

30. D - Elizabeth

3

WOMEN PIRATES

Answers for this chapter on page 61

1. Her bloody reign made her public enemy #1 with the government of her country.

    A. Jacquette Delahaye   B. Cheng I Sao

    C. Queen Teuta of Illyria   D. Jeanne de Clisson

2. From 1515 to 1542 she controlled the western part of the Mediterranean Sea.

    A. Sayyida al-Hurra   B. Grace O'Malley

    C. Mary Read   D. Queen Teuta of Illyria

3. She had taken on a job as a merchant sailor disguised as a male and turned pirate when buccaneers attacked the ship she was working on.

    A. Anne Bonny   B. Cheng I Sao

    C. Mary Read   D. Jeanne de Clisson

Women In History Trivia

4. She was one of the first and only American women to try her hand at piracy.

    A. Queen Teuta of Illyria   B. Jacquette Delahaye

    C. Anne Bonny   D. Rachel Wall

5. She was one of the earliest known female pirates in history who lived in 3rd century B.C.

    A. Cheng I Sao   B. Sayyida al-Hurra

    C. Queen Teuta of Illyria   D. Jeanne de Clisson

6. Chieftain of a clan of Ireland in the 16th century, she fought fearlessly for the independence of Ireland against the English crown and controlled the coastlines through intimidation and plunder as a pirate.

    A. Grace O'Malley   B. Anne Bonny

    C. Mary Read   D. Rachel Wall

7. One of history's most influential women pirates began her life in a Chinese brothel.

    A. Queen Teuta of Illyria   B. Sayyida al-Hurra

    C. Mary Read   D. Cheng I Sao

8. She became a pirate to take revenge on the French King Philip VI after her husband was executed for treason. She bought three warships and she and her crew terrorized the English Channel capturing only French ships and killing the crew.

A. Jeanne de Clisson   B. Jacquette Delahaye

   C. Rachel Wall   D. Grace O'Malley

9. She retired as one of history's most successful pirates.

   A. Grace O'Malley   B. Cheng I Sao

   C. Queen Teuta of Illyria   D. Rachel Wall

10. She married a sailor and journeyed to a pirate-infested island in the Bahamas where she fell under the spell of 'Calico Jack,' a buccaneer. She proved she could wield a pistol and cutlass with the best of the crew.

   A. Anne Bonny   B. Rachel Wall

   C. Jacquette Delahaye   D. Jeanne de Clisson

11. She became the last woman ever executed in Massachusetts when she was hanged to death.

   A. Sayyida al-Hurra   B. Mary Read

   C. Rachel Wall   D. Jeanne de Clisson

12. She reigned over the Adriatic Sea attacking Roman and Greek ships.

   A. Cheng I Sao   B. Grace O'Malley

   C. Sayyida al-Hurra   D. Queen Teuta of Illyria

Women In History Trivia

13. Born in Haiti, she was a pirate who lived in the 17th century.

    A. Jeanne de Clisson   B. Anne Bonny

    C. Jacquette Delahaye   D. Rachel Wall

14. She was a pirate, queen, and ally of the infamous Turkish pirate Barbarossa.

    A. Queen Teuta of Illyria B. Cheng I Sao

    C. Grace O;Malley   D. Sayyida al-Hurra

15. What two female pirates joined up together and played a leading role in a spree of raids? When captured they both dodged the noose when it was discovered they were both pregnant.

    A. Anne Bonny   B. Mary Read

    C. Rachel Wall   D. Jacquette de Clisson

16. After the death of her husband she took power and plundered her way across Southeast Asia and assembled a fleet that rivaled many country's navies.

    A. Queen Teuta of Illyria B. Cheng I Sao

    C. Sayyida al-Hurra   D. Grace O'Malley

17. Daughter of a wealthy nobleman and sea trader, she inherited her father's shipping business. She commanded hundreds of men and twenty ships in raids on rival clans and merchant ships.

A. Anne Bonny   B. Jacquette Delahaye

C. Mary Read   D. Grace O'Malley

18. She was not only a pirate but the ruler of Moroccan city Tetouan and later married the king of Morocco.

A. Jacquotte Delahaye   B. Rachel Wall

C. Sayyida al-Hurra   D. Queen Teuta of Illyria

Answers - Chapter 3 – Women Pirates

1. B- Cheng I Sao

*When not only the Chinese were fighting her but also the British and the Portuguese navies were brought in to bring her to justice, she agreed to lay down her cutlass in exchange for the right to keep all her ill-gotten gains. She retired from the life of a pirate and ran a gambling house until her death.

2. A- Sayyida al-Hurra

3. C- Mary Read

4. D- Rachel Wall

5. C- Queen Teuta of Illyria

6. A- Grace O'Malley

7. D- Cheng I Sao

8. A- Jeanne de Clisson

9. B- Cheng I Sao

10. A- Anne Bonny

11. C- Rachel Wall

12. D- Queen Teuta of Illyria

13. C- Jacquette Delahaye

14. D- Sayyida al-Hurra

15. A & B- Anne Bonny & Mary Read

16. B- Cheng I Sao

*She along with her husband, before his death, ran one of China's most formidable pirate armies with hundreds of ships and 50,000 men.

17. D- Grace O'Malley

*One of few seafaring families on the west coast, the family owned castles facing the sea to protect their territory. They attacked ships, plundered Scotland's islands, and taxed those who fished off their coasts. They would board the ships and demand cash or cargo for safe passage.

18. C- Sayyida al-Hurra

4

WOMEN OF EARLY AMERICAN HISTORY

Late 1500's – late 1800's

Answers for this chapter on page 76

1. Her parents were among the 120 settlers who left England in 1587 on an expedition sponsored by Sir Walter Raleigh, sailing on the ship *The Lion.* The group of settlers landed on Roanoke Island. She was born on the island.

    A. Elizabeth Hopkins

    B. Virginia Dare

    C. Dorothy Bradford

    D. Eleanor Creesy

2. She saved the life of John Smith and other English settlers by warning them of an ambush.

    A. Sacajawea

    B. Tituba

    C. Minnie Hollow Wood

    D. Pocahontas

3. She was the first woman to set foot on the Plymouth Rock as the Pilgrims left the Mayflower in 1620.

A. Elizabeth Hopkins   B. Mary Chilton Winslow

C. Priscilla Mullins Alden   D. Pocahontas

4. Shoshone Indian and wife to the guide and interpreter Lewis and Clark hired to explore the lands acquired in the Louisiana Purchase, she was the only woman in the 'Voyage of Discovery.'

A. Minnie Hollow Wood   B. Marie Tallchief

C. Sacajawea   D. Buffalo Bird Woman

5. I imagine there isn't an American who hasn't heard about Betsy Ross, but can you name the woman who sewed the flag that flew over Fort McHenry, the flag that Francis Scott Key would spot as he wrote 'The Star Spangled Banner'?

A. Mary Pickersgill   B. Virginia Dare

C. Sarah Edmonds   D. Eleanor Creesy

6. Early spring in 1692 began the infamous Salem witch trials. She was the first convicted witch who was hung.

A. Sybilla Masters   B. Sarah Borginis

C. Bridget Bishop   D. Eleanor Creesy

7. She is regarded as the first American born baby.

A. Resolved White   B. Oceanus Hopkins

C. Jemima Boone   D. Virginia Dare

8. A passenger on the Mayflower, while anchored off Provincetown Harbor while the men were on land seeking a place to build their colony she fell off the Mayflower into the freezing waters and drowned.

    A. Priscilla Mullins Alden   B. Dorothy Bradford

    C. Julia Grant   D. Lucy Brewer

9. Finding herself at the age of sixteen responsible for one of her family's plantations in the South, she experimented with different crops to see what would grow best in the Southern climate and soil. From seeds her father sent her from the French West Indies she changed agriculture in colonial South Carolina where she developed indigo as one of it's most important cash crops.

    A. Adelicia Acklen   B. Anneke Lockermans Van Courtland

    C. Eliza Lucas   D. Mary Pickersgill

10. Nearly all the survivors of the Alamo were women. She is the most well-known of them and the sole adult Anglo survivor.

    A. Susanna Dickinson   B. Sarah Edmonds

    C. Eleanor Creesy   D. Eliza Lucas

11. Wife of one of the most famous generals of the Civil War, she was also the great granddaughter of Martha Washington.

    A. Clara Barton   B. Hannah Penn

    C. Lucy Brewer   D. Mary Custis Lee

12. She is the most well-known woman who came to America on the Mayflower, in large part due to Henry Wadsworth Longfellow's poem 'The Courtship of Miles Standish.'

   A. Elizabeth Hopkins   B. Priscilla Mullins Alden

   C. Dorothy Bradford   D. Pocahontas

13. After the outbreak of the Revolutionary War violence increased between the Indians and the settlers in Kentucky. The Indians raided the settlements in hopes to drive the settlers away. In July of 1776, a raiding party took captive three teenage girls from Boonesborough. One of the girls was the daughter of the American pioneer famous for his exploration and settlement of Kentucky. He along with a rescue party safely returned the girls home. Who was the young daughter of this legend?

   A. Mary Allerton   B. Eliza Lucas

   C. Jemima Boone   D. Priscilla Mullins Alden

14. After the death of her famous Quaker husband who was founder of the North American colony of Pennsylvania, she became most likely the only woman who ever became feudal proprietor of such an immense domain, the province of Pennsylvania.

   A. Jemima Boone   B. Geraldine Lucas

   C. Marion Sloan   D. Hannah Penn

15. We'll call it a legend since it hasn't been proven one way or another; but it's said she admitted to different people after the event that she had been in the barn at the time when one of her cows kicked over a lantern starting the Chicago Fire of 1871. In a sworn affidavit she swore she was in bed when the fire started.

A. Katie O'Leary   B. Lucy Brewer

C. Bridget Bishop   D. Eliza Lucas

16. After the Civil War ended she worked for the War Department helping to reunite soldiers with their families or discover more on those who were missing; which included identifying the dead at Andersonville prison.

A. Clara Barton   B. Julia Grant

C. Elizabeth Blackwell D. Bridget Bishop

17. She was the daughter of Powhatan, a chief of the Powhatan empire. Just a young Native American girl about ten to twelve years of age, she helped to bring about peace between the Jamestown settlers and the Native Americans.

A. Jemima Boone   B. Pocahontas

C. Minnie Hollow Wood   D. Sacajawea

18. Born in the early 1700's, at sixteen years of age she became responsible for managing one of her family's plantations along with it's twenty slaves in the Carolinas. Her letter book where she kept meticulous records is one of the most impressive collections of personal writings of an 18th century woman giving great insight into life on a plantation.

A. Eliza Lucas   B. Anneke Lockermans Van Courtland

C. Adelicia Acklen   D. Sarah Borginis

19. There were a number of children among the passengers of the

Mayflower. She was four years old when she sailed on the Mayflower and would become the last surviving Mayflower passenger.

    A. Susanna White   B. Virginia Dare

    C. Dorothy Bradford   D. Mary Allerton

20. She was taken prisoner aboard an English ship to be used as an exchange of prisoners along with tools and weapons that had been stolen from the English by the Indians. During her captivity she converted to Christianity, was baptized, and changed her name to Rebecca. She would later marry an Englishman who came to Jamestown by the name of John Rolfe, a tobacco planter.

    A. Jemima Boone   B. Pocahontas

    C. Minnie Hollow Wood   D. Priscilla Mullins Alden

21. During the Civil War she went to the front to tend to the sick and wounded without being paid for her services.

    A. Bridget Bishop   B. Susanna Dickinson

    C. Clara Barton   D. Julia Grant

22. She received the first patent issued to man or woman in American history.

    A. Sybilla Masters   B. Sarah Borginis

    C. Charley Parkhurst   D. Eleanor Creesy

23. When she sailed on the Mayflower with her husband she had a

daughter around two years of age, Damaris. Her second child, Oceanus, was born aboard the Mayflower on it's journey to America.

    A. Priscilla Mullins Alden   B. Mary Allerton

    C. Elizabeth Hopkins   D. Susanna White

24. She invented a way to clean and refine Indian corn the colonists grew in early America.

    A. Sarah Borginis   B. Marion Sloan

    C. Sybilla Masters   D. Lucy Brewer

25. In 1648 this woman of New Amsterdam, tired of the dust and mud in front of her home paved the first street in America – or rather she supervised as her servants covered the road with cobblestones.

    A. Adelicia Acklen   B. Hannah Penn

    C. Eliza Lucas   D. Anneke Lockermans Van Courtland

26. She was founder and first president of the American Red Cross.

    A. Clara Barton   B. Elizabeth Hopkins

    C. Sarah Edmonds   D. Eleanor Creesy

27. Her father, one of the oldest Mayflower passengers, died while the Mayflower was docked at Provincetown Harbor. Her mother died the first winter leaving this thirteen-year-old girl an orphan

in a new land.

    A. Elizabeth Hopkins   B. Geraldine Lucas

    C. Mary Chilton Winslow   D. Priscilla Mullins Alden

28. The question of what happened to her, the first born white settler in the New World remains a mystery.

    A. Susanna White   B. Virginia Dare

    C. Mary Norris Allerton   D. Pocahontas

29. What was turned into burial grounds during the Civil War was first the home of the great-granddaughter of Martha Washington. This great-granddaughter married a man in that very home who would later become a famous general of the Civil War. Her father, grandson to Martha Washington, built the home on land he had inherited from his grandmother. Wife of the famous general, she had to abandon the home during the war as the Union army was about to occupy the property. This property later became Arlington Cemetery. Who was the wife of the general whose home this was?

    A. Mary Custis Lee   B. Julia Grant

    C. Hannah Penn   D. Julia Grant Cantacuzene

30. During the War of 1812, serving aboard 'Old Ironsides' as George Baker he was actually a woman. The Marine Corps reluctantly later admitted that she was perhaps the very first female Marine.

    A. Minnie Hollow Wood   B. Lucy Brewer

    C. Charley Parkhurst   D. Tituba

31. More than 400 women disguised themselves as men and fought during the Civil War. One of the first documented female soldiers was this woman who joined the army under the alias of Frank Thompson.

    A. Sarah Edmonds   B. Sarah Borginis

    C. Geraldine Lucas   D. Sybilla Masters

32. She was one of the wealthiest women in the antebellum South. Cousin to Rutherford B. Hayes, wife of a wealthy businessman and plantation owner, when widowed at a young age she inherited seven Louisiana cotton plantations, a 2,000 acre farm in Tennessee, and hundreds of slaves all valued at over a million dollars. After her husband's death she managed everything herself and did a very good job of it.

    A. Elizabeth Blackwell   B. Anneke Lockermans Van Courtland

    C. Hannah Penn   D. Adelecia Acklen

33. One of the only four women to have survived to celebrate the 'First Thanksgiving,' she became a widow. Her second marriage was the first marriage to take place at Plymouth.

    A. Dorothy Bradford   B. Susana White

    C. Clara Barton   D. Eliza Lucas

34. One of the most famous stagecoach drivers during the 1850's and 1860's was not a man, but this woman. Her true identity wasn't discovered until after her death. When neighbors came to prepare 'his' body for burial they discovered he was a she.

A. Marion Sloan   B. Sybilla Masters

C. Eleanor Creesy   D. Charley Parkhurst

35. Young girls accused of witchcraft in the Salem witch trials accused this woman of being the one who bewitched them.

A. Anneke Lockermans Van Courtland   B. Sarah Borginis

C. Tituba   D. Minnie Hollow Wood

36. After her father's death she came across her father's memoirs of his days growing up at Mount Vernon. She organized her father's papers and had them made into a book. In 1859, she completed this project and it was published as, 'Recollections and Private Memoirs of Washington, by His Adopted Son George Washington Parke Custis, With A Memoir of this Author By His Daughter.' Who was his daughter?

A. Julia Grant Cantacuzene   B. Mary Custis Lee

C. Priscilla Mullins Alden   D. Geraldine Lucas

37. She enlisted with her husband during the Mexican American War. She served as cook until the Mexicans began bombarding Fort Texas (Fort Brown) at which time she was issued a musket. She never missed her mark and General Zachary Taylor, a future president, breveted her to colonel making her the first female colonel of the U.S. Army.

A. Sarah Borginis   B. Julia Grant

C. Susana Dickinson   D. Sarah Edmonds

38. Her entire family died the first winter at Plymouth and she

then lived with the Brewster family. She married, had eleven children, and became one of the founders of Duxbury, Massachusetts.

 A. Elizabeth Blackwell   B. Priscilla Mullins Alden

 C. Mary Chilton Winslow   D. Hannah Penn

39. In 1852, this seven year-old came to Santa Fe in a covered wagon with her brother and mother. After a street urchin stole her mother's purse with all their money in it they traveled no further than Santa Fe (they had originally planned to continue on as far as California). When the young girl went to school she was the only student who spoke English. Her childhood memories include a boy who was bitten by a mad dog and later died and making the acquaintance of Kit Carson.

 A. Bridget Bishop   B. Sarah Borginis

 C. Marion Sloan   D. Eleanor Creesy

40. This plantation owner managed to save her crop of cotton from being burned to keep it out of the hands of Union soldiers during the Civil War by doing some fast talking. She soon sold the cotton to Rothschild of London for $960,000 in gold. Quite a coup, as the price of cotton in the South at the time was next to nothing.

 A. Eliza Lucas   B. Geraldine Lucas

 C. Adelicia Acklen   D. Eleanor Creesy

41. She was a Lakota woman who earned the right to wear a warbonnet due to her valor at the Battle of Little Big Horn.

| A. Sacajawea | B. Marie Tallchief |
| C. Pocahontas | D. Minnie Hollow Wood |

42. When this woman's husband saw Santa Ana arrive, he scooped his wife and daughter up and ran them to the mission (the Alamo) just before the Mexican army opened fire. She spent most of the battle at the Alamo hiding in a small room with her baby daughter. Her husband was killed during the battle but she and her infant daughter survived. General Santa Ana while interviewing the survivors days after the battle offered to adopt her daughter and give her a good education. She refused his offer and he set mother and child free.

| A. Susana Dickinson | B. Jemima Boone |
| C. Sybilla Masters | D. Mary Pickersgill |

43. As a young child she was a passenger on the Mayflower. She would in later years marry a passenger from the ship 'Fortune,' the second English ship to arrive at Plymouth. She and her husband had eight children, seven of which survived to adults, and fifty grandchildren. Both she and her husband lived to an old age.

| A. Sybilla Masters | B. Mary Allerton |
| C. Priscilla Mullins Alden | D. Susanna White |

44. When she was about twelve years of age she had been captured by Hidatsa warriors. She was later purchased from the tribe by a French-Canadian fur trapper.

| A. Sacajawea | B. Pocahontas |
| C. Charley Parkhurst | D. Eleanor Creesy |

45. She came on the Mayflower with her husband William who died the first winter along with their son Resolved. She gave birth to son Peregrine while the Mayflower was still anchored off Cape Cod.

    A. Susanna White   B. Sarah Borginis

    C. Mary Allerton   D. Virginia Dare

Answers - Chapter 4 – Women of Early American History

1. B - Virginia Dare

2. D - Pocahontas

3. B - Mary Chilton Winslow

*Tradition states she raced John Alden to the front of the launch bringing the Mayflower passengers to shore. She was the first to step off the boat and the first to set foot on Plymouth Rock.

4. C - Sacajawea

*She was a Shoshone wife to the man Lewis & Clark hired as their guide and interpreter.

5. A - Mary Pickersgill

*Mary was a flag maker living in Baltimore. Her mother had been a flag maker during the Revolutionary War and taught her daughter who carried on the profession. Mary had a flag shop and catered to the military. In 1813 the city of Baltimore was preparing for an eventual British attack. Major Armistead, commander of the militia stationed at Fort McHenry, ordered a garrison flag "so large that the British will have no difficulty seeing it from a distance." Mary Pickersgill was commissioned to make two flags: a 17' x 25' flag and a garrison flag 30' x 42'. It was too large a job for Mary to undertake on her own so she hired five other women to aid her in the task. It took them six weeks to complete the order. The flag weighed fifty pounds and took nine men to hoist the flag over the fort. When the Battle of Baltimore took place the flag was flying, the very flag Francis Scott Key spotted while being held on a British ship while there to exchange prisoners. It was there where he wrote 'The Star Spangled Banner' while he watched the battle through the night. Mary Pickersgill made that star spangled banner that can be currently seen at the Smithsonian Institution in Washington, D.C.

6. C - Bridget Bishop

7. D - Virginia Dare

8. B - Dorothy Bradford

9. C - Eliza Lucas

10. A - Susanna Dickinson

11. D - Mary Custis Lee

12. B - Priscilla Mullins Alden

13. C - Jemima Boone

14. D - Hannah Penn

15. A - Kate (Catherine) O'Leary

*The fire burned for two days. Up to 300 people were killed by the fire, more than 100,000 were left homeless, and 3.3 sq. miles of Chicago burned.

16. A - Clara Barton

17. B - Pocahontas

18. A - Eliza Lucas

19. D - Mary Allerton

20. B - Pocahontas

*She would later marry an Englishman by the name of John Rolfe who came to Jamestown. He was a tobacco planter.

21. C - Clara Barton

*While tending the wounded at the Battle of Antietam, she worked so close to the battlefield that a bullet went through her sleeve killing the man she was treating.

22. A - Sybilla Masters

*She received the patent in 1715. The invention was a way to clean and refine Indian corn. Her innovation processed the corn into different food and cloth products. Though it was her discovery, at the time it was unlawful by the British courts (this was when America were still British colonies) for women or minorities to have the right to own a patent so it was put in her husband's name, Thomas Masters.

23. C - Elizabeth Hopkins

24. C -Sybilla Masters

25. D -Anneke Lockermans Van Courtland

26. A -Clara Barton

27. C -Mary Chilton (Winslow)

*She lived with the families of Miles Standish for a time and with the family of John Alden after the death of her parents.

28. B -Virginia Dare

*The mystery lies in not only what happened to Virginia Dare, but to the entire colony of English settlers. They all vanished never to have been discovered as to what happened to them. The only sign left behind was the word "Croatoan" carved on a wooden post. Did it mean that the settlers were attacked by the local Croatoan Indian tribe or had they departed for nearby Croatoan Island? Before White could dispatch a search party to Croatoan Island, a hurricane forced the expedition to sail for England. In 1937 Louis Hammond while out hunting hickory nuts near Edenton, North Carolina found a stone with a strange inscription he couldn't identify. He took the stone to have it examined by history professor, Dr. Haywood Pearce of Emory University. Dr. Pearce identified the inscription as being Elizabethan English and determined that the stone was a written record of what had happened to the "Lost Colony". Forty-six more stones were found during the next few years. Whether valid or not as to coming from the Lost Colony is yet to be determined, but at least the first stone is given credence by many historians giving historians a better idea of what may have happened to the Lost Colony.

29. A -Mary Custis Lee

30. B -Lucy Brewer

31. A -Sarah Edmonds

*She served as a male nurse and a spy. Once she passed herself off as a black laundry woman and surprised her superiors with confederacy papers she discovered in an officer's jacket. After the war she wrote the bestseller, 'Nurse and Spy In The Union Army.'

32. D -Adelecia Acklen

33. B - Susanna White (Winslow)

34. D - Charley Parkhurst

35. C - Tituba

*She was the Parris family's Caribbean slave. Two other women were also accused for this offense; Sarah Good a homeless beggar and Sarah Osborne an elderly, impoverished woman.

36. B - Mary Custis Lee

37. A - Sarah Borginis

38. B - Priscilla Mullins Alden

39. C - Marion Sloan

40. C - Adelicia Acklen

41. D - Minnie Hollow Wood

42. A - Susanna Dickinson

43. B - Mary Allerton

44. A - Sacajawea

45. A - Susanna White

5

WOMEN OF THE AMERICAN REVOLUTION

Answers for this chapter on page 91

1. Her numerous letters to her husband, a founding father who was serving in the Continental Congress, informed many of the founding fathers of what was occurring in the colonies and of the mindset of the colonists. Her letters in later years gave historians great insight on what life was like in the colonies during this time.

    A. Abigail Adams   B. Martha Washington

    C. Mercy Otis Warren   D. Peggy Shippen Arnold

2. Her husband was Commander of the Continental Army in the Revolutionary War.

    A. Nancy Hart   B. Abigail Adams

    C. Lucy Knox   D. Martha Washington

3. She has been one of the nation's best-known figures of the American Revolution, a patriotic icon. We have been taught in our history books that she was the woman George Washington went to for her to sew the first American flag. It is said that it was her

idea the stars should be five-pointed. Yet today, historians claim there is no compelling evidence to prove this. They don't argue the fact that she probably did sew the first American flag for Washington, though they are less convinced she instigated any change in the design in the flag. Whether legend or truth to the story, she remains a symbol of patriotism in our nation's history.

    A. Margaret Corbin   B. Sybil Ludington

    C. Betsy Ross   D. Molly Pitcher

4. Recently freed from indentured servitude on a farm when the Revolutionary War broke out, she wanted to do her part to aid in the war effort. She bound her chest, dressed like a man, and enlisted in the Fourth Massachusetts Regiment under the name of Robert Shurtleff. It was only years later when she fell deathly ill that while examining her a doctor discovered the truth.

    A. Deborah Samson   B. Molly Pitcher

    C. Sarah Fulton   D. Nancy Ward

5. She is given credit for the idea of the men disguising themselves as Mohawk Indians during the Boston Tea Party.

    A. Abigail Adams   B. Esther Reed

    C. Anna Maria Lane   D. Sarah Fulton

6. Mary Ludwig said to have brought soldiers pitchers of water as they fought, earned her legendary status in history when during the Battle of Monmouth her husband collapsed and she took his place at the cannon. She is more popularly remembered with what moniker?

A. Peggy Shippen Arnold   B. Molly Pitcher

C. Mercy Otis Warren   D. Sybil Ludington

7. Her spying career saved thousands of lives of Revolutionary soldiers, including the life of General Washington.

A. Lydia Darragh   B. Prudence Cummings Wright

C. Catherine Moore Berry   D. Peggy Shippen Arnold

8. She was an influential writer, the first woman playwright, was the first man or woman to write the first history of the American Revolutionary War, and influenced the founding fathers.

A. Martha Washington   B. Abigail Adams

C. Mercy Otis Warren   D. Nancy Ward

9. Much more than just the wife of a founding father and future president, she made a name for herself in her war contributions, such as making ammunition for the soldiers.

A. Lucy Knox   B. Abigail Adams

C. Betsy Ross   D. Peggy Shippen Arnold

10. She gained notoriety for being the highest paid spy in the American Revolutionary War and was wife to history's most infamous traitor.

A. Molly Brant   B. Esther Reed

C. Anna Maria Lane   D. Peggy Shippen Arnold

11. As a nurse she followed her husband into the American Revolutionary War. Having closely watched her husband she knew how to fire, clean, and aim the cannon so when he was killed she took his place until she too was hit and wounded. She was completely disabled, and Congress recognizing her valor and sacrifice approved the granting of a lifetime soldier's half-pay pension for her.

    A. Lucy Knox   B. Margaret Corbin

    C. Sarah Fulton   D. Molly Brant

12. She was the first documented female to serve as a soldier.

    A. Nancy Ward   B. Molly Pitcher

    C. Anna Maria Lane   D. Prudence Cummings Wright

13. When news was received the British were attacking Danbury, Connecticut, the local militia needed to be informed in order to stop the British. In the middle of the night she rode about forty miles in a rainstorm shouting for the militia to assemble. About four hundred troops responded to her call.

    A. Sybil Ludington   B. Betsy Ross

    C. Margaret Corbin   D. Deborah Samson

14. She fought in the Revolutionary War for three years before it was discovered she was a girl. When her true identity was discovered she was given an honorable discharge and given enough money to get home. She demanded back pay for her service and Congress voted to grant her pension as a war veteran. She has been declared Massachusetts' official state heroine.

A. Sarah Fulton	B. Deborah Samson
C. Sybil Ludington	D. Mercy Otis Warren

15. As head of the women's militia in her town when she discovered her Tory brother along with others were smuggling information to Boston, in order to prevent the British in Boston from learning about American troop movements she and the other women militia members captured them, recovered their documents, and held them prisoner proving how valuable the women's assistance in the war effort was. Who was this leader of the militia who captured her own brother and the other spies?

A. Abigail Adams	B. Nancy Hart
C. Lydia Darragh	D. Prudence Cummings Wright

16. During the Revolutionary War, the British instilled the Quartering Act making the colonists provide them with housing and food. When her home was used as a gathering place for British officers, she would hide in a closet and spy on the officers learning their strategies. She then passed that info on to the Continental Army. This forewarning included plans for a surprise attack against troops led by General Washington. The warning enabled them to fight off the attack. Who was this spy?

A. Agent 355	B. Lydia Darragh
C. Agent 007	D. Peggy Shippen Arnold

17. One of the most mysterious figures of the American Revolution was a member of the Culpepper Spy Ring. After more than 200 years her identity is still unknown, she is known only as a number.

A. Agent 355   B. Agent 93

C. Lucy Knox   D. Peggy Shippen Arnold

18. Her husband was involved in the patriotic movement, fought in the beginning of the Revolutionary War, became president of the Massachusetts House of Representatives, Speaker of the House, and President of the Massachusetts Provincial Congress. With all his accomplishments, he realized it was his wife who could speak and write better than he. His involvement in the patriotic movement inspired her to write for which she became famous.

A. Lucy Knox   B. Abigail Adams

C. Mercy Otis Warren D. Deborah Samson

19. Wife of a Revolutionary General she, along with her husband often dined with the likes of George Washington and John Adams. Her husband away at war she stayed behind in Philadelphia to raise their six children and aid the soldiers. She formed the Ladies of Philadelphia who went door to door and collected over $300,000. With the money the Ladies of Philadelphia purchased linen and sewed over 2,000 shirts for the soldiers.

A. Esther Reed   B. Martha Washington

C. Prudence Cummings Wright   D. Lucy Knox

20. An excellent equestrian she knew all the trails and shortcuts near her South Carolina plantation so was an excellent choice as a scout for the American army.

A. Sybil Ludington   B. Lydia Darragh

C. Nancy Ward   D. Catherine Moore Barry

21. During the Battle of Bunker Hill she took her son, who would later become a president, to witness this historic event.

    A. Lucy Knox   B. Martha Washington

    C. Abigail Adams   D. Betsy Ross

22. The British laid siege to Boston. Aware of a shipment of wood meant for the American troops she discovered it was confiscated by the British. This woman pursued the British soldiers, grabbed the oxen by the horns pulling the wagon load of firewood, and turned them around leading them back to Boston. The British soldiers threatened to shoot. She merely told them to "shoot away." The British were so astonished by the brave act of this woman they let her go – and the firewood too. Who was this woman?

    A. Agent 355   B. Sarah Fulton

    C. Molly Brant   D. Abigail Adams

23. She was a Mohawk and her people were a part of the Iroquois Confederacy. Companion or common-law wife to Sir William she was a Loyalist. She was also a spy for the Loyalists.

    A. Molly Brant   B. Nancy Ward

    C. Anna Maria Lane   D. Lydia Darragh

24. She stayed with her husband, Commander of the American Continental Army, at Valley Forge every winter. She endeared hardships at the winter quarters and tirelessly sewed for the men, nursed their wounds, and encouraged the soldiers bringing great comfort to them.

A. Lucy Knox   B. Martha Washington

C. Peggy Shippen Arnold   D. Mercy Otis Warren

25. One fearless woman was able to out-smart six British soldiers when they arrived at her cabin demanding information on a man they were searching for. Little did they know when they shot her turkey and ordered her to cook it for them that she would soon be holding them captive. She and her daughter confiscated their weapons, warned the neighbors, and shot and killed one soldier who tried to retrieve their weapons. In the end, she and her husband saw to it they were hung and buried in their backyard. Who was this brave woman?

A. Nancy Hart   B. Abigail Adams

C. Molly Brant   D. Catherine Moore Barry

26. This agent of the Culper Spy Ring may have been a maid in a well-regarded Loyalist family in New York City or even possibly a family member. Whoever she was, her information was quite detailed and helped to uncover General Benedict Arnold's plans to betray the Revolutionary Army. It is said she was later captured by the British and held on a prisoner ship where she died. Whoever she was, she gave great detailed information and even George Washington wasn't privy as to her identity.

A. Agent 1776   B. Deborah Samson

C. Agent 355   D. Peggy Shippen Arnold

27. In a leadership role she held among the Cherokees one of her responsibilities was to watch over the prisoners. During the French and Indian War the Cherokees had aided the British and continued to do so throughout the Revolutionary War. This

Cherokee woman however sided with the colonists. When she learned of a coming attack on the colonists she freed the prisoners so they could warn the settlers. After the war she helped negotiate peace with the new United States.

    A. Nancy Ward

    B. Molly Brant

    C. Margaret Corbin

    D. Sybil Ludington

28. She was responsible for convincing women to volunteer to nurse and tend to wounded soldiers. She found an open space and set up working as surgeon to the wounded soldiers.

    A. Lucy Knox

    B. Abigail Adams

    C. Betsy Ross

    D. Sarah Fulton

29. Before the war her husband was a book store owner. He may be most remembered for retrieving the cannons from Fort Ticonderoga, a major feat. She came from a Loyalist family and made the difficult choice to turn her back on her family. As an officer's wife she chose to support her husband and the soldiers of the Continental army and camped at Valley Forge throughout the winters along with Martha Washington and other officers' wives. She served the men tirelessly by nursing them back to health.

    A. Martha Washington

    B. Lucy Knox

    C. Esther Reed

    D. Anna Maria Lane

30. While her husband was away, a founding father and member of the Second Continental Congress, she homeschooled her children, ran the farm, housed many refugees fleeing from Boston, and joined others who questioned the Massachusetts women residents to see if they were loyal Patriots or Tories to enlighten the founding

fathers as to the mindset of those back home.

    A. Mercy Otis Warren   B. Betsy Ross

    C. Martha Washington   D. Abigail Adams

31. What Quaker woman whose home was often used for a meeting place for the British officers smuggled the plans of the British troops, often sewn into button covers or needle books to her son who served in the Revolutionary army?

    A. Lydia Darragh   B. Esther Reed

    C. Sarah Fulton   D. Betsy Ross

32. She helped organize a donation campaign to aid the soldiers and their needs. She personally donated $20,000 of her own money, a very large sum for that time.

    A. Catherine Moore Berry   B. Prudence Cummings Wright

    C. Martha Washington   D. Abigail Adams

33. Historians suspect that she was the link between Revolutionary's most infamous traitor and British spy Major John Andre.

    A. Peggy Shippen Arnold   B. Agent 355

    C. Lydia Darragh   D. Nancy Hart

34. She was the first woman in U.S. history to receive a pension from Congress for military service due to no longer being able to

walk after receiving an injury during the war.

 A. Margaret Corbin   B. Molly Brant

 C. Molly Pitcher   D. Sarah Fulton

35. She was inducted into the Woman's Hall of Fame in Seneca Falls, N.Y. in 2002. She is said to have supplied political parties with their arguments, she was the first woman in America who wrote of state policy and history.

 A. Abigail Adams   B. Deborah Samson

 C. Mercy Otis Warren   D. Catherine Moore Barry

Answers - Chapter 5 – Women of the American Revolution

1. A -Abigail Adams

2. D- Martha Washington

3. C- Betsy Ross

*Why is it we learned in history class for almost 250 years that Betsy Ross was the one who made our nation's first flag and now all these years later that fact seems to be in dispute? This is in large part due to the fact that the records of the U.S. flag's origins are fragmentary, in part because at the time Americans didn't look upon flags as national relics. You wouldn't think it would be that way considering this was the first flag of a new nation, but it appears there was more at stake at the time than making a written notation of who sewed the flag. So, Betsy's creation of the flag is not an established historical fact like the signing of the Declaration of Independence and there is no flag that actually exists that is said to have been the flag sewn by Betsy Ross. There is no available evidence sufficient to establish Betsy as the creator of the flag with certainty. There is an affidavit given by her daughter describing the events of George Washington coming to their home asking her mother to sew the flag. It isn't unusual that Betsy Ross would be chosen to do so. She prayed in the pew next to George Washington and had already sewn for him in the past, and the fact that she was a niece of George Ross (one of the signers of the Declaration of Independence), it is not exceptional that these members of the Flag Committee formed by the Continental Congress would call upon her to make the flag. So, is it an indisputable fact that she sewed the flag? No, but evidence certainly leans that way.

4. A -Deborah Samson

*Deborah Samson was injured in battle several times, always refusing medical care for fear her secret would be discovered. In 1783, she became very ill to the point of death. A doctor checked the soldier's pulse, then rested a hand on his chest to see if he was still breathing. He was – and the doctor was surprised to discover the soldier wasn't a man at all, but a woman who had bound her chest and disguised herself to become a soldier.

5. D -Sarah Fulton

6. B - Molly Pitcher

7. A - Lydia Darragh

8. C - Mercy Otis Warren

9. B - Abigail Adams

*The army finally received what they had been requesting for so long: weapons. Although they received muskets, they quickly discovered they did not come with bullets or gun powder; leaving them defenseless. Abigail Adams came to the rescue. She went home immediately, gathered all the silver and steel in the house, melted it down, and with the help of her children made bullets for the army. After seeing the bravery of this woman patriot the army was heartened for the first time in a long while. This act of loyalty gave inspiration to those in the army.

10. D - Peggy Shippen Arnold

11. B - Margaret Corbin

12. C - Anna Maria Lane

13. A - Sybil Ludington

14. B - Deborah Samson

15. D - Prudence Cummings Wright

16. B - Lydia Darragh

17. A - Agent 355

18. C - Mercy Otis Warren

19. A - Esther Reed

20. D - Catherine Moore Barry

21. C - Abigail Adams

22. B - Sarah Fulton

23. A - Molly Brant

24. B -Martha Washington

25. A -Nancy Hart

*The British soldiers entered the cabin and stacked their weapons in a corner demanding something to drink. Hart obliged them by serving them wine. As the soldiers drank, Hart with the pretense of sending her daughter to the spring for water secretly instructed her daughter to blow a conch shell kept hidden nearby to alert the neighbors. As Hart served the soldiers and passed between them and their weapons she began to pass the muskets through an opening in the cabin wall to her daughter who was outside. When the soldiers noticed what was going on they rushed to retrieve their weapons. She warned them she would shoot any man that moved. Ignoring her warning, one man made the deadly mistake of approaching her. She shot him and held the rest off until her husband and others arrived. Her husband wanted to shoot the remaining hostages but she insisted on hanging them in order to reserve the precious ammunition and not to be overheard by possibly other soldiers.

In 1912, workmen grading a railroad near the site of the old Hart cabin unearthed a neat row of six skeletons that lay under nearly three feet of earth and were estimated to have been buried for at least a century.

26. C -Agent 355

27. A -Nancy Ward

28. D -Sarah Fulton

29. B -Lucy Knox

30. D -Abigail Adams

31. A -Lydia Darragh

32. C -Martha Washington

33. A -Peggy Shippen Arnold

34. A -Margaret Corbin

35. C -Mercy Otis Warren

6

AMERICAN CIVIL RIGHTS ACTIVISTS

Answers for this chapter on page 101

1. She called for an amendment to the U.S. Constitution giving women the right to vote. Her efforts helped bring about the eventual passage of the 19th Amendment, giving all citizens the right to vote.

    A. Margaret Fuller   B. Elizabeth Cady Stanton

    C. Margaret "Molly" Brown   D. Dorothea Dix

2. An escaped slave herself, she made several trips back to the south to aid other slaves to freedom, helped abolitionist John Brown recruit men for his raid on Harper's Ferry, served as a scout and a spy during the Civil War, and was an activist in the fight for women's suffrage.

    A. Susan B. Anthony   B. Gloria Steinem

    C. Sojourner Truth   D. Harriet Tubman

3. She became one of the most famous 19th century black women in

America. An uneducated former slave who spoke out against slavery. Not knowing how to read or write, she used her words becoming a moving speaker for black freedom and women's rights. While most of the black abolitionists spoke only to blacks, she spoke to the whites. While others spoke of violent uprisings, she spoke of reason and religious understanding.

    A. Sojourner Truth   B. Rosa Parks

    C. Harriet Tubman   D. Dorothea Dix

4. She was the leading American female abolitionist in 1840.

    A. Margaret Fuller   B. Elizabeth Cady Stanton

    C. Lucretia Mott   D. Susan B. Anthony

5. She was the first woman to run for Congress. Though barred from voting she knew there was no law preventing her from taking national office if elected.

    A. Margaret "Molly" Brown   B. Elizabeth Cady Stanton

    C. Margaret Fuller   D. Dorothea Dix

6. In 1872 she voted in the presidential election, an illegal act for a woman. She was duly arrested for her actions.

    A. Susan B. Anthony   B. Lucretia Mott

    C. Dorothea Dix   D. Elizabeth Cady Stanton

7. In 1955 she refused to surrender her bus seat to a white passenger, which brought about the Montgomery boycott and other efforts to end segregation.

    A. Lucretia Mott   B. Rosa Parks

    C. Sojourner Truth   D. Dorothea Dix

8. In 1932 she received the French Legion of Honour for her efforts during and after the sinking of the Titanic, for her work with children, her work on behalf of miners' rights, and her volunteer work during WWI.

    A. Dorothea Dix   B. Lucretia Mott

    C. Elizabeth Cady Stanton   D. Margaret "Molly" Brown

9. She was one of the leading voices of the abolitionist and feminist movements and as a Quaker adopted their anti-slavery viewpoint. She helped form the Philadelphia Female Anti-Slavery Society in 1833 and was one of the founders of the American womens' rights movements. She helped establish Swarthmore College and served as head of the American Equal Rights Association.

    A. Margaret Fuller   B. Elizabeth Cady Stanton

    C. Lucretia Mott   D. Susan B. Anthony

10. She was an early leader of the womens' rights activists and wrote the Declaration of Sentiment as a call to arms for female equality.

Women In History Trivia

    A. Susan B. Anthony   B. Harriet Tubman

    C. Elizabeth Cady Stanton   D. Sojourner Truth

11. She was an American abolitionist, born into slavery who escaped and led several rescue missions leading other slaves to their freedom in what is known as the Underground Railroad.

    A. Rosa Parks   B. Harriet Tubman

    C. Lucretia Mott   D. Sojourner Truth

12. She was in the forefront fighting for women to have the right to vote. It wasn't until 14 years after her death that the 19th Amendment was passed. In recognition of her hard work on the subject her portrait was put on the one dollar coins in 1979 making her the first woman to be so honored.

    A. Dorothea Dix   B. Elizabeth Cady Stanton

    C. Lucretia Mott   D. Susan B. Anthony

13. Her book 'Woman In The Nineteenth Century,' is considered the first major feminist work in the U.S.

    A. Margaret Fuller   B. Elizabeth Cady Stanton

    C. Gloria Steinem   D. Susan B. Anthony

14. Her arm was dislocated by a streetcar conductor who refused to let her, a black woman ride. She would fight for and win the

rights for blacks to ride in streetcars.

    A. Rosa Parks   B. Harriet Tubman

    C. Margaret "Molly" Brown   D. Sojourner Truth

15. She was president of the National Women Suffrage Association for twenty years.

    A. Lucretia Mott   B. Dorothea Dix

    C. Elizabeth Cady Stanton   D. Susan B. Anthony

16. During the Civil War she worked for the Union Army as a cook, nurse, armed scout, and spy. She was the first woman to lead an armed expedition in the war, guided the Combahee River Raid liberating more than 700 slaves in South Carolina.

    A. Harriet Tubman   B. Margaret Fuller

    C. Gloria Steinem   D. Dorothea Dix

17. She was a reformer whose efforts on behalf of the mentally ill and prisoners helped create new institutions across the U.S. and Europe.

    A. Margaret Fuller   B. Dorothea Dix

    C. Lucretia Mott   D. Susan B. Anthony

18. She was an African-American abolitionist and womens' rights activist who had been born into slavery but escaped to freedom in

1826.

    A. Harriet Tubman   B. Sojourner Truth

    C. Rosa Parks   D. Gloria Steinem

19. She was one of the first women in the U.S. to run for political office. Between 1909 – 1914 before women had the right to vote she made several unsuccessful bids for a seat in Congress. She was involved in the early feminist movement and helped establish the Colorado Chapter of the National American Woman's Suffrage Association.

    A. Margaret "Molly" Brown   B. Elizabeth Cady Stanton

    C. Lucretia Mott   D. Susan B. Anthony

20. She was a pioneer crusader for the women's suffrage movement in America and president of the National American Woman Suffrage Association.

    A. Margaret Fuller   B. Dorothea Dix

    C. Susan B. Anthony   D. Elizabeth Cady Stanton

21. She held the famous Seneca Falls Convention in 1848 with Lucretia Mott and several other women where they proposed that women be granted the right to vote.

    A. Dorothea Dix   B. Elizabeth Cady Stanton

    C. Margaret Fuller   D. Susan B. Anthony

22. She was among the founders of the National Women's Political Caucus, the feminist *Ms.* Magazine, and an outspoken champion of women's rights.

    A. Gloria Steinem   B. Margaret Fuller

    C. Lucretia Mott   D. Susan B. Anthony

23. She received many accolades during her lifetime, including the NAACP's highest awards. She became a nationally recognized symbol of dignity and strength in the struggle to end entrenched racial segregation. She became known as "The Mother of the Civil Rights Movement."

    A. Susan B. Anthony   B. Elizabeth Cady Stanton

    C. Rosa Parks   D. Gloria Steinem

24. She became well-known for her improvised speech on racial inequalities, "*Ain't I A Woman?*" delivered at the Ohio Women's Rights Convention in 1851.

    A. Rosa Parks   B. Harriet Tubman

    C. Lucretia Mott   D. Sojourner Truth

25. After the Civil War she worked to secure the franchise and educational opportunities for freedmen. She had also opened her home to runaway slaves escaping via the Underground Railroad.

    A. Sojourner Truth   B. Lucretia Mott

    C. Margaret "Molly" Brown   D. Dorothea Dix

Answers - Chapter 6 – American Civil Rights Activists

1. B -Elizabeth Cady Stanton

2. D -Harriet Tubman

3. A -Sojourner Truth

4. C -Lucretia Mott

5. B -Elizabeth Cady Stanton

6. A -Susan B. Anthony

7. B -Rosa Parks

8. D -Margaret "Molly" Brown

9. C -Lucretia Mott

10. C -Elizabeth Cady Stanton

11. B -Harriet Tubman

*She led hundreds of enslaved people to freedom along the route of the Underground Railroad earning the nickname of 'Moses.'

12. D -Susan B. Anthony

13. A -Margaret Fuller

14. D -Sojourner Truth

15. C -Elizabeth Cady Stanton

16. A -Harriet Tubman

17. B - Dorothea Dix

18. B - Sojourner Truth

*At the age of 9 she was sold at an auction along with a flock of sheep for $100 for the entire lot.

19. A - Margaret "Molly" Brown

20. C - Susan B. Anthony

21. B - Elizabeth Cady Stanton

22. A - Gloria Steinem

23. C - Rosa Parks

24. D - Sojourner Truth

*The first version of this speech was published in an Ohio newspaper, 'The Anti-Slavery Bugle.' The statement, 'Ain't I A Woman?' wasn't even mentioned. It was 12 years later before this phrase was even heard as 'a Southern-tinged version of the speech.' It's highly unlikely that Sojourner Truth, a native of New York whose first language was Dutch would have ever used this Southern slang.

25. B - Lucretia Mott

7

THEY DID IT FIRST

Answers for this chapter on page 109

1. She was the first woman on the United States Supreme Court.

    A. Lillian Bland   B. Jacqueline Cochran

    C. Valentina Tereshkova   D. Sandra Day O'Connor

2. She was the first person to fly solo from Hawaii to the American mainland.

    A. Geraldine Mock   B. Diane Crump

    C. Amelia Earhart   D. Svetlana Savitskaya

3. She is the first woman in the world to have flown in space.

    A. Geraldine Mock   B. Jacqueline Cochran

    C. Sally Ride   D. Valentina Tereshkova

4. In 1979 she became Britain's first female prime minister.

A. Margaret Thatcher   B. Elizabeth Windsor

C. Ada Lovelace   D. Victoria Woodhull

5. She became the first U.S. female astronaut in space.

   A. Lillian Bland   B. Sally Ride

   C. Valentina Tereshkova   D. Sandra Day O'Connor

6. In 1909, this 22-year old made history as the first woman to drive across the U.S.

   A. Alice Ramsey   B. Aloha Wanderwell

   C. Diane Crump   D. Anna Rainsford French Bush

7. She was the first female war reporter on the front lines in WWI.

   A. Mary Patten   B. Ann Bancroft

   C. Nellie Bly   D. Gertrude Ederle

8. In 1911 she became the first woman to design, build, and fly an aircraft.

   A. Margaret Wright   B. Lilian Bland

   C. Amelia Earhart   D. Jacqueline Cochran

9. She was the first woman hanged by the federal government.

Women In History Trivia

    A. Mary Surratt   B. Nellie Bly

    C. Victoria Woodhull   D. Ann Bancroft

10. In 1856 when her husband took ill, she took command of his ship 'The Neptune's Car' and his crew en route from Europe to San Francisco. For fifty-six days this eighteen year old pregnant wife of the captain successfully navigated the ship around Cape Horn to off the coast of Chile.

    A. Junko Tabei   B. Aloha Wanderwell

    C. Mary Patten   D. Alice Ramsey

11. In 1975 she became the first woman to reach the summit of Mount Everest and the first woman to ascend all Seven Summits by climbing the highest peak on every continent.

    A. Tina Sjögren   B. Svetlana Savitskaya

    C. Valentina Tereshkova   D. Junko Tabei

12. She was the first woman to ride in the Kentucky Derby.

    A. Alice Ramsey   B. Ann Davison

    C. Diane Crump   D. Mary Patten

13. She became the first woman to receive a license to drive a car.

    A. Victoria Woodhull   B. Geraldine Mock

    C. Gertrude Ederle   D. Anna Rainsford French Bush

14. She became the first woman to break the sound barrier.

    A. Sally Ride   B. Jacqueline Cochran

    C. Lilian Bland   D. Mary Patten

15. She was the first woman to win a Nobel Prize.

    A. Amelia Earhart   B. Tina Sjögren

    C. Marie Curie   D. Sally Ride

16. In 1926 she became the first woman to swim across the English Channel.

    A. Alice Ramsey   B. Gertrude Ederle

    C. Diane Crump   D. Laura Dekker

17. In 1984 she became the first woman to walk in space.

    A. Valentina Tereshkova   B. Lilian Bland

    C. Sally Ride   D. Svetlana Savitskaya

18. She was the youngest, not only female but person, at age 16 to complete her solo circumnavigation around the globe single-handed.

    A. Laura Dekker   B. Ann Davison

    C. Victoria Woodhull   D. Mary Patten

19. She was the first woman to fly around the world.

    A. Lilian Bland

    B. Diane Crump

    C. Geraldine Mock

    D. Amelia Earhart

20. She was the first woman to reach the North Pole by foot and dogsled.

    A. Ann Bancroft

    B. Svetlana Savitskaya

    C. Tina Sjögren

    D. Junko Tabei

21. From 1952 – 1953 she became the first woman to cross the Atlantic solo in a sailboat.

    A. Laura Dekker

    B. Gertrude Ederle

    C. Ann Davison

    D. Ann Bancroft

22. She is recognized as the first computer programmer.

    A. Alice Ramsey

    B. Ada Lovelace

    C. Diane Crump

    D. Margaret Thatcher

23. She was the first woman to complete the Three Poles Challenge – climb Mount Everest and reach both the North and the South Pole.

    A. Junko Tabei

    B. Ann Bancroft

    C. Valentina Tereshkova

    D. Tina Sjögren

24. She was the first woman to run for the United States President (in 1872).

   A. Geraldine Mock

   B. Sandra Day O'Connor

   C. Victoria Woodhull

   D. Ann Bancroft

25. She was the first woman to drive around the world.

   A. Diane Crump

   B. Alice Ramsey

   C. Lilian Bland

   D. Aloha Wonderwell

Answers - Chapter 7 – They Did It First

1. D - Sandra O'Connor

2. C - Amelia Earhart

3. D - Valentina Tereshkova

4. A - Margaret Thatcher

5. B - Sally Ride

6. A - Alice Ramsey

7. C - Nellie Bly

8. B - Lilian Bland

9. A - Mary Surratt

*She was hanged for conspiring with John Wilkes Booth in the assassination of President Lincoln.

10. C - Mary Patten

11. D - Junko Tabei

12. C - Diane Crump

13. D - Anne Rainsford French Bush

*She actually obtained a "steam engineer's license," which entitled her to operate a "four-wheeled vehicle powered by steam or gas."

14. B - Jacqueline Cochran

15. C - Marie Curie

16. B - Gertrude Ederle

17. D - Svetlana Savitskaya

18. A -Laura Dekker

* New Zealand born, Dutch sailor at age 13 she sailed solo from the Netherlands to England and back. She wanted to begin her world voyage at age 14 but was stopped by the courts. She was still able to complete her world voyage by the age of 16.

19. C -Geraldine Mock

20. A -Ann Bancroft

21. C -Ann Davison

22. B -Ada Lovelace

*Her father was Lord Byron.

23. D -Tina Sjögren

24. C -Victoria Woodhull

25. D -Aloha Wanderwell

*Her birth name was Idris Galcia Hall, but she changed her first name to Aloha during the journey and married the sponsor of the Challenge and took on his last name. It was an endurance race between two teams in Ford Model T's to see who could visit the most countries. Joining the expedition while still a teenager she traveled through 43 countries on four continents. In her memoirs she recounts French battlefields, Mussolini's Italy, mobs in Germany desperate for food after WWI, camping beneath the Great Sphinx in Egypt, and witnessing Jews building a new nation in Palestine. Later in life she befriended a native tribe in Bororo in Brazil after her plane went down in uncharted jungle territory. She made a documentary film of their life, the first ever filmed record of the Bororeo tibe, an important anthropological document. That film today can be seen at the Smithsonian, 'Flight To The Stone Age Bororos.'

8

FEMME FATALES
&
BADASS WOMEN

Answers for this chapter on page 118

1. She was one of the most famous women gangsters in all history.

    A. Pearl Elliott   B. Stephanie St. Clair

    C. Bonnie Parker   D. Mary "Stagecoach" Fields

2. She was known as "The Flamingo," as well as "Queen of the Gangster Molls." Bugsy Siegel named his Las Vegas hotel, The Flamingo, after her.

    A. Virginia Hill   B. Helen Gillis

    C. Charlotte Corday   D. Laura Bullion

3. She ran a boardinghouse in Washington, D.C. which became a meeting place for John Wilkes Booth and his fellow conspirators where they plotted to kill the president. She was involved in their conversations and concealed their weapons.

A. Pearl Elliott   B. Mary Surratt

C. Stephanie St. Clair   D. Bonnie Parker

4. She was an assassin at the age of twenty-five. Daughter of French nobles during the French Revolution, she set her sights on Jean-Paul Marat a leader of the French Revolution and stabbed him to death in his own bathtub for which she was sent to the guillotine.

A. Boudica   B. Stephanie St. Clair

C. Charlotte Corday   D. Virginia Hill

5. This badass woman was no gangster's moll. She ran a brothel and was a member of the notorious Dillinger gang. She was on Chicago Police's Public Enemy List in 1933.

A. Helen Gillis   B. Virginia Hill

C. Laura Bullion   D. Pearl Elliott

6. A Dutchwoman with an unhappy marriage behind her she reinvented herself as an exotic dancer dancing in transparent, revealing costumes with a jeweled bra and extraordinary headpiece. This femme fatale was acknowledged as the most glamorous and desirable woman in Paris who was often seen with aristocrats, diplomats, financiers, top military officers, and wealthy businessmen. During WWI she became a spy and was later tried and executed.

A. Mata Hari   B. Boudica

C. Delilah   D. Pandora

7. A temptress from the Old Testament, she is a Philistine who betrays Samson into revealing his secret that where his extreme strength came from was his long hair.

    A. Eve   B. Pandora

    C. Delilah   D. Cleopatra

8. She was killed in a shootout with FBI agents in 1935.

    A. Helen Gillis   B. Ma Barker

    C. Belle Starr   D. Mata Hari

9. She was convicted of horse stealing along with other crimes in the late 1800's. She served time in a federal penitentiary before being shot and killed on her ranch.

    A. Mary "Stagecoach" Fields   B. Laura Bullion

    C. Bonnie Parker   D. Belle Starr

10. She drank whiskey, smoked cigars, toted a shotgun, and wasn't a woman you wanted to mess with having the reputation of the toughest badass in Montana. This former slave, at the age of sixty, was hired by the U.S. Postal Service becoming the second woman and the first black woman to work as a mail carrier.

    A. Pearl Elliott   B. Mary Surratt

    C. Mary "Stagecoach" Fields   D. Ma Barker

11. She exposed corrupt cops by placing ads in leading newspapers about the bribes she gave them and then testified against them.

A. Bonnie Parker   B. Helen Gillis

C. Pearl Elliott   D. Stephanie St. Clair

12. She became notorious as the girlfriend of Brooklyn mobster Bugsy Siegel becoming his lover and courier.

    A. Helen Gillis   B. Virginia Hill

    C. Charlotte Corday   D. Mata Hari

13. Her life was cut short dying at the age of twenty-three in a police shootout.

    A. Bonnie Parker   B. Ma Barker

    C. Laura Bullion   D. Stephanie St. Clair

14. After her husband king of a British Celtic tribe known as Iceni died, the Romans claimed the Iceni tribe were now under their rule. She declared war in response and rode her chariot leading the army herself. The Roman army was too powerful to defeat, but for centuries she has been a legend for having the courage to stand up against the Roman army with her female warriors.

    A. Pandora   B. Mata Hari

    C. Boudica   D. Delilah

15. She was tried and found guilty of conspiracy to kill President Lincoln. She became the first woman to be sentenced to death by the United States.

A. Belle Starr   B. Pearl Elliott

C. Charlotte Corday   D. Mary Surratt

16. She was an outlaw in the 19th Century. She was married to a Cherokee Indian and together they housed outlaws on their ranch and lived a bandit's life preying on travelers and cowboys passing through the area.

A. Mary "Stagecoach" Fields   B. Belle Starr

C. Laura Bullion   D. Helen Gillis

17. She was a numbers runner in Harlem in the 1920's. She went to war with notorious Jewish gangster Dutch Schultz over the Harlem gambling territory which she considered her neighborhood.

A. Virginia Hill   B. Charlotte Corday

C. Ma Barker   D. Stephanie St. Clair

18. Not any different from others in her position during those times but perhaps because she is more well-known, she is looked on as a femme fatale by using her charms to lure both Julius Caesar and Marc Anthony. She then had them come to her aid in leading a revolt against her brother/husband she co-ruled with leading to his death and had a second brother/husband she co-ruled with killed in order to reestablish her power on the Egyptian throne.

A. Delilah   B. Pandora

C. Cleopatra   D. Boudica

19. She belonged to the Wild Bunch Gang with Butch Cassidy and the Sundance Kid.

    A. Laura Bullion   B. Bonnie Parker

    C. Ma Barker   D. Mary "Stagecoach" Fields

20. This woman of ancient Greek mythology was the first woman on earth created by a male god. She is infamous for opening the box (or jar) that let all the evil into the world.

    A. Delilah   B. Pandora

    C. Mata Hari   D. Cleopatra

21. She was described by J. Edgar Hoover as "the most dangerous criminal brain of the last decade."

    A. Stephanie St. Clair   B. Bonnie Parker

    C. Helen Gillis   D. Ma Barker

22. During WWI both Germany and France approached her to spy for them. She turned Germany down but took the money they offered. The Frenchman who recruited her to spy for France is the same one who later turned her in for being a German spy. She was executed by a firing squad even though the prosecution later confessed, "There was not enough evidence to flog a cat in the case."

    A. Charlotte Corday   B. Helen Gillis

    C. Stephanie St. Clair   D. Mata Hari

23. She was an active member of the Wild Bunch Gang and was jailed for being involved in the Great Northern train robbery of 1901.

    A. Laura Bullion   B. Bonnie Parker

    C. Ma Barker   D. Mary "Stagecoach" Fields

24. At sixteen years of age she married Lester Gillis who was later known as Baby Face Nelson. By the age of twenty her name was added to the "shoot to kill" list, even though she was regarded more as an accomplice than a gangster.

    A. Mary "Stagecoach" Fields   B. Belle Starr

    C. Laura Bullion   D. Helen Gillis

25. She was involved in a string of bank, store, and gas station robberies across the U.S. in the years 1932 – 1934.

    A. Ma Barker   B. Bonnie Parker

    C. Pearl Elliott   D. Virginia Hill

Answers - Chapter 8 – Femme Fatales & Badass Women

1. C - Bonnie Parker

2. A - Virginia Hill

*She grew up poor telling people she didn't have a pair of shoes until she was seventeen. She moved to Chicago seeking fame and fortune and initially became an accountant for Al Capone which introduced her to the gangster world.

3. B - Mary Surratt

4. C - Charlotte Corday

5. D - Pearl Elliott

6. A - Mata Hari

7. C - Delilah

8. B - Ma Barker

9. D - Belle Starr

10. C - Mary "Stagecoach" Fields

11. D - Stephanie St. Clair

12. B - Virginia Hill

13. A - Bonnie Parker

*She was half of the iconic crime duo, Bonnie & Clyde. Killed in a shootout at the age of 23, Clyde was also killed at age 25 in the shootout.

14. C - Boudica

15. D - Mary Surratt

16. B - Belle Starr

17. D -Stephanie St. Clair

18. C -Cleopatra

19. A -Laura Bullion

20. B -Pandora

21. D -Ma Barker

22. D -Mata Hari

23. A -Laura Bullion

24. D -Helen Gillis

25. B -Bonnie Parker

9

FAMOUS WOMEN AUTHORS

Answers for this chapter on page 127

1. British novelist known for her Harry Potter series, while very much alive and still writing so not exactly a part of history 'yet,' but after winning multiple awards and selling millions of copies the books have become the best-selling books in history. Who is this famous author?

    A. Margaret Mitchell   B. Emily Dickinson

    C. J.K. Rowling   D. Laura Ingalls Wilder

2. Her book 'Uncle Tom's Cabin' which depicted the harsh conditions for enslaved African Americans was said to have played an important role in the Civil War. The book having raised the ire of southerners and brought about fierce debate from others, it was also said that President Lincoln only half-joking said she held some responsibility for starting the Civil War.

    A. Louisa May Alcott   B. Harper Lee

    C. Zora Neale Hurston   D. Harriet Beecher Stowe

3. This Jewish German-born diarist became one of the most well-known victims of the Holocaust once the book, 'The Diary of a Young Girl' came out which was a journal of her experiences from 1942 – 1944 during the war.

    A. Ayn Rand   B. Anne Frank

    C. Pearl Buck   D. Agatha Christie

4. She was an American novelist best known as the author of 'Little Women' and it's sequels.

    A. Laura Ingalls Wilder   B. Margaret Mitchell

    C. Emily Dickinson   D. Louisa May Alcott

5. She has earned the title 'Queen of Mystery' as one of the best-selling authors in history.

    A. Agatha Christie   B. Emily Dickinson

    C. J.K. Rowling   D. Maya Angelou

6. She published only one book for half a century, but that book made such an impact dealing with racial inequality and injustice that she was awarded the Presidential Medal of Freedom for her contribution in literature.

    A. Harriet Beecher Stowe   B. Maya Angelou

    C. Harper Lee   D. Zora Neale Hurston

7. She became one of the most famous women in the 19th Century when her poem was first published.

A. Beatrix Potter   B. Pearl Buck

C. Emily Dickinson   D. Julia Ward Howe

8. She was a reclusive American poet unrecognized in her own lifetime. She secretly wrote hundreds of poems and letters which her sister found after her death. She is known for her poignant and compressed verse. She is considered one of the towering figures of American literature.

A. Emily Dickinson   B. Pearl Buck

C. Lucy Maud Montgomery   D. Katharine Lee Bates

9. She was a Russian-born American writer whose works, 'The Fountainhead' and 'Atlas Shrugged' are based on her political views and emphasis on individual rights.

A. Maya Angelou   B. Beatrix Potter

C. Ayn Rand   D. Charlotte Brontë

10. She published four novels and more than fifty published short stories, plays, and essays. She is best known for her novel 'Their Eyes Were Watching God.' She is an American folklorist and writer associated with the Harlem Renaissance who celebrated the African American culture of the rural South. She herself, grew up in Eatonville, Florida; the first incorporated all-black town in the country.

A. Pearl Buck   B. Zora Neale Hurston

C. Harriet Beecher Stowe D. Maya Angelou

11. 'Anne of Green Gables' brought what author instant fame?

   A. Lucy Maud Montgomery   B. Emily Dickinson

   C. Margaret Mitchell   D. Emily Brontë

12. She is an English novelist and poet, one of three sisters who were all writers. She wrote 'Jane Eyre,' which was published in 1847, a classic of English literature.

   A. Agatha Christie   B. Emily Dickinson

   C. Emily Brontë   D. Charlotte Brontë

13. She wrote the poem 'America the Beautiful' which was first published in 1893. The poem later became the lyrics to the patriotic ballad we still sing with pride well over one hundred years after she wrote it.

   A. Julia Ward Howe   B. Katharine Lee Bates

   C. Lucy Maud Montgomery   D. Harriet Beecher Stowe

14. In a series of children's books, she wrote of her life as a young girl living on the American prairie in the late 1800's titled 'The Little House' series.

   A. Anne Frank   B. Louisa May Alcott

   C. Laura Ingalls Wilder   D. Beatrix Potter

15. An American writer, she was the daughter of missionaries who spent most of her life in China. In 1938, she was awarded the Nobel Prize in Literature "for her rich and truly epic descriptions

of peasant life in China and for her biographical masterpieces."

    A. Emily Dickinson   B. Lucy Maud Montgomery

    C. Lucy Maud Montgomery   D. Pearl Buck

16. She is best known for her series of autobiographies focusing on her childhood and early adult experiences, the first of which was, 'I Know Why The Caged Bird Sings,' which brought her international recognition and acclaim.

    A. Maya Angelou   B. Pearl Buck

    C. Harper Lee   D. Zora Neale Hurston

17. An English novelist and poet, she is best known for her only novel 'Wuthering Heights,' a classic of English literature.

    A. Emily Dickinson   B. Emily Brontë

    C. Agatha Christie   D. Charlotte Brontë

18. She became one of the most famous writers in history with mysteries such as, 'Murder On The Orient Express,' which helped her become appointed Dame Commander of the Order of the British Empire for her contribution to literature.

    A. J.K. Rowling   B. Margaret Mitchell

    C. Agatha Christie   D. Charlotte Brontë

19. This British author is one of the most beloved children's authors of all times. Her children's books star characters Peter Rabbit, Jemima Puddle-Duck, and Benjamin Bunny.

A. Beatrix Potter   B. Laura Ingalls Wilder

C. Pearl Buck   D. Lucy Maud Montgomery

20. This American novelist grew up among many well-known authors such as: Ralph Waldo Emerson, Nathaniel Hawthorne, Henry David Thoreau, and Henry Wadsworth Longfellow. Before writing her most famous children's series she wrote lurid and violent tales. She volunteered as a nurse in the Civil War and later received her first fame from writing, 'Hospital Sketches,' a publication of her letters in book form. Her children's book, 'Little Women' was autobiographical.

A. Margaret Mitchell   B. Emily Dickinson

C. Harriet Beecher Stowe   D. Louisa May Alcott

21. She was the first American woman to win the Nobel Prize for literature. Her novel 'The Good Earth' was the best-selling fiction book in the U.S. in 1931 and 1932 and won the Pulitzer Prize in 1932.

A. Emily Dickinson   B. Katharine Lee Bates

C. Pearl Buck   D. Zora Neale Hurston

22. She was active in the Civil Rights Movement and worked with Martin Luther King, Jr. and Malcolm X. She recited her poem, 'In The Pulse of Morning' at President Clinton's inauguration, becoming the first to make an inaugural recitation since Robert Frost at President Kennedy's inauguration.

A. Maya Angelou   B. Zora Neale Hurston

C. Lucy Maud Montgomery   D. Harriet Beecher Stowe

23. This author whose well-known book *Gone With The Wind* about the Civil War in Atlanta is the fourth-generation Atlanton. Her great-great-great grandfather fought in the American Revolutionary War, his son took part in the War of 1812, while her grandfather fought in the Civil War.

    A. Emily Dickinson   B. Margaret Mitchell

    C. Julia Ward Howe   D. Lucy Maud Montgomery

24. She was the author of *Uncle Tom's Cabin*, the best-selling novel of the 19th Century about anti-slavery.

    A. Emily Dickinson   B. Katharine Lee Bates

    C. Harper Lee   D. Harriet Beecher Stowe

25. She is an American novelist known for her 1960 Pulitzer Prize winning book *To Kill A Mocking Bird*. The book was an autobiographical book of what she saw as a child growing up in the south about racism.

    A. Harper Lee   B. Maya Angelou

    C. Zora Neale Hurston   D. Katharine Lee Bates

Answers - Chapter 9 – Famous Women Authors

1. C -J.K. Rowlings

*This British author claims to have been homeless before her books were published, but now is richer than the Queen of England and lives in a home that looks like a castle fit for a queen.

2. D -Harriet Beecher Stowe

3. B -Anne Frank

*The book has also been published under the name 'The Diary of Anne Frank.' Fleeing Nazi persecution during WWII, she was fifteen years old when her family was found hiding in a space at the back of her father's company building. Employees provided food until two years later they were betrayed and arrested. It has never been discovered to this day who it was who betrayed them. The family were sent to concentration camps where Anne Frank died along with her entire family other than her father. Her diary was later published by her father, the only one of his family to survive the concentration camps.

4. D -Louisa May Alcott

5. A -Agatha Christie

*A British author, she is famous for her seventy detective novels with fictional detectives Poirot and Miss Marple.

6. C -Harper Lee

7. D -Julia Ward Howe

*The poem was set to an old folk tune used for 'John Brown's Body.' The poem later turned song was written after visiting an Army camp during the Civil War and was considered the Union's most popular song. The song was 'Battle Hymn of the Republic.'

8. A -Emily Dickinson

9. C -Ayn Rand

*She became an American citizen in 1931. Her novels promoting individualism and laissez-faire capitalism were influential among the young from the mid-20th Century.

10. B -Zora Neale Hurston

11. A -Lucy Maud Montgomery

12. D - Charlotte Brontë

13. B -Katherine Lee Bates

14. C -Laura Ingalls Wilder

15. D -Pearl Buck

16. A -Maya Angelou

17. B -Emily Brontë

18. C -Agatha Christie

19. A -Beatrix Potter

20. D -Louisa May Alcott

21. C -Pearl Buck

22. A -Maya Angelou

23. B -Margaret Mitchell

*At her request, upon her death the original manuscript was burned other than a few pages retained to validate her authorship.

24. D -Harriet Beecher Stowe

25. A -Harper Lee

10

FAMOUS WOMEN ARTISTS

Answers for this chapter on page 136

1. She was an American folk artist who began painting in earnest at the age of 78.

    A. Georgia O'Keefe   B. Grandma Moses

    C. Mary Cassatt   D. Joan Mitchell

2. She has been recognized as the "Mother of American Modernism."

    A. Georgia O'Keefe   B. Anna Ancher

    C. Judith Leyster   D. Grandma Moses

3. She was a painter from France who was a part of the painters in France known as the Impressionists.

    A. Louise Élisabeth Vigée Le Brun   B. Caterina van Hemessen

    C. Giovanni Garzoni   D. Berthe Moriset

4. This French artist is best known as a portrait painter from the Rococo period. She was the personal portrait painter of Marie Antoinette and her royal family. Not only did she paint 600 portraits in her lifetime, but she also painted 200 landscapes.

    A. Caterina van Hemessen   B. Louise Élisabeth Vigée Le Brun

    C. Suzanne Valadon   D. Berthe Moriset

5. This Polish Art Deco artist was one of the most sought after society painters. During the Roaring Twenties she could command a good price for a portrait and some of those who sat for her were kings and queens.

    A. Levina Teerlinc   B. Anna Ancher

    C. Frida Kahlo   D. Tamara de Lempicka

6. A second-generation abstract Expressionist, this Chicago-born artist held the record for most-expensive painting by a female artist, (her painting sold for $11.9 million in 2011) before being surpassed by Georgia O'Keefe in 2014.

    A. Anna Ancher   B. Judith Leyster

    C. Joan Mitchell   D. Mary Cassatt

7. This 17th century artist was one of the first women to paint still life. She was official court painter for the Grand Duke Ferdinando II and the Medici family were patrons of her art.

    A. Giovanni Garzoni   B. Elisabetta Sirani

    C. Sofonisba Anguissola   D. Artemisia Gentileschi

8. She was an Italian Baroque painter who rose to prominence in the 17th century despite the hostility towards women artists at the time. Her father was also a professional painter who greatly influenced her work. Art critics often stated it's difficult to distinguish between the two. She carved a name for herself as one of the leading painters and most influential artists of the era. 'Judith Slaying Holofernes' is one of her most famous works.

    A. Giovanni Garzoni   B. Artemisia Gentileschi

    C. Tamara de Lempicka   D. Yayoi Kusamen

9. She was an American painter and printmaker. She lived much of her adult life in France. She often created images of the social and private lives of women and many of her paintings featured mothers and children.

    A. Georgia O'Keefe   B. Mary Cassatt

    C. Berthe Moriset   D. Grandma Moses

10. She was a Mexican painter best known for her self-portraits. Her work has been celebrated in Mexico as emblematic of national and indigenous tradition. Mexican culture and Amerindian cultural traditions were important aspects of her work.

    A. Frida Kahlo   B. Suzanne Valadon

    C. Levina Teerlinc   D. Elisabetta Sirani

11. Born in New York she studied at Oberlin, one of the first colleges in the U.S. to admit women and people of color. She faced discrimination during her education, including being beaten and being accused of poisoning her classmates. She pursued sculptures and spent most of her artistic career in Rome. She is best known

for her 3,015 pound marble sculpture, 'The Death of Cleopatra.'

    A. Giovanni Garzoni   B. Anna Ancher

    C. Yayoi Kusamen   D. Edmonia Lewis

12. This Dutch female painter was the first female painter to be registered to the Haarlem Guild of St. Luke. This artist from the 1600's is most well-known for her 'Self-Portrait.'

    A. Artemisia Gentileschi   B. Caterina van Hemessen

    C. Judith Leyster   D. Edmonia Lewis

13. Her family strongly objected to her painting and when she announced her plans to paint in Paris her father declared he'd rather see her dead than living abroad as a bohemian. She went anyway; however with her father's words in mind she submitted one of her paintings to a prestigious Paris salon under another name.

    A. Mary Cassatt   B. Anna Ancher

    C. Judith Leyster   D. Joan Mitchell

14. She was completely self-taught, but it didn't impede her from becoming one of the most famous folk artists of the 20th century.

    A. Edmonia Lewis   B. Grandma Moses

    C. Judith Leyster   D. Yayoi Kusamen

15. In the 1500's, this Flemish artist created portraits of Elizabeth I, many in miniatures. The Victoria and Albert Museum in London

declared her responsible for inventing royal miniatures.

    A. Levina Teerlinc   B. Anna Ancher

    C. Tamara de Lempicka   D. Suzanne Valadon

16. A Japanese artist who became bored with the traditional painting of her ancestry moved to New York and often shared gallery exhibit space with Andy Warhol. Her work encompassed pop art, minimalism, and feminist art movements. She is known for her dotted, large landscapes. She returned to Japan and admitted herself to a mental hospital where she still lives today. She still works at her studio daily which is a short distance from the mental hospital where she lives.

    A. Frida Kahlo   B. Judith Leyster

    C. Artemisia Gentileschi   D. Yayoi Kusamen

17. She was one of the first female painters to achieve worldwide acclaim from critics and the public. An American artist, she is best known for her paintings of enlarged flowers, New York skyscrapers, and New Mexico landscapes.

    A. Mary Cassatt   B. Georgia O'Keefe

    C. Judith Leyster   D. Grandma Moses

18. An Italian painter of the 1600's, even though she died in her twenties by that time she had already created over 200 paintings. Her Baroque paintings had dramatic dark backdrops with vibrant colors with depictions of powerful heroines.

    A. Sofonisba Anguissola   B. Caterina van Hemessen

    C. Elisabetta Sirani   D. Suzanne Valadon

19. French painter who regularly modeled for Henri De Toulouse-Lautree, Pierre-Auguste Renoir, and Edgar Degas, she taught herself how to paint at the age of nine. She was a trapeze artist before modeling and after ten years painted instead of being painted.

    A. Louise Élisabeth Vigée Le Brun   B. Sofonisba Auguissola

    C. Berthe Morisot   D. Suzanne Valadon

20. A painter herself, she was painted by Manet at least eleven times. Friends with Manet, she met and married his brother who was also a painter. She befriended other artists such as Degas and Bazille. Her grandfather was the influential Rococo painter Jean-Honoré Fragonard. While she was not commercially successful in her lifetime, she still outsold Monet, Renoir, and Sisley.

    A. Berthe Morisot   B. Caterina van Hemessen

    C. Giovanni Garzoni   D. Berthe Moriset

21. This Italian painter from the 1500's was of noble descent whose unofficial mentor was Michelangelo. She received great opportunities due to her wealth and status, but was denied many possibilities as an artist because she was a woman.

    A. Louise Élisabeth Vigée Le Brun   B. Sofonisba Anguissola

    C. Giovanni Garzoni   D. Caterina van Hemessen

22. She is considered one of the best contemporary Indigenous Australian artists. She was declared a "State Living Treasure," the year of her death (1998).

Women In History Trivia

    A. Yayoi Kusamen   B. Anna Ancher

    C. Frida Kahlo   D. Queenie McKenzie

23. She is considered one of Denmark's great pictorial artists. As a painter she was a pioneer in realistic art involving the interplay of colors in natural light. Most of her paintings were of Skagen (Skagen is an area in northern Denmark) women doing chores.

    A. Suzanne Teerlinc   B. Anna Ancher

    C. Edmonia Lewis   D. Judith Leyster

24. While her work varied between the literal portraits, abstractions, and landscapes; her work is still most identified by her iconic flower paintings. In 2014 one of her floral paintings sold for $44 million, setting the record for artwork by a female artist.

    A. Grandma Moses   B. Mary Cassatt

    C. Georgia O'Keefe   D. Berthe Moriset

25. Flemish Renaissance painter from the 1500's, she is most known for having been the first painter to create a self-portrait depicting an artist at their easel.

    A. Caterina van Hemessen   B. Elisabetta Sirani

    C. Suzanne Valadon   D. Tamara de Lempicka

Answers - Chapter 10 – Famous Women Artists

1. B -Grandma Moses

It was in 1938 when an art collector saw a few of her paintings hanging in a store window that he purchased them all. The next day he visited the artist at her home and bought all the paintings she had. Her first one woman show was held in New York in 1940 and she immediately became famous.

2. A -Georgia O'Keefe

3. D -Berthe Moriset

4. B -Louise Élisabeth Vigée Le Brun

5. D -Tamara de Lempicka

6. C -Joan Mitchell

7. A -Giovanni Garzoni

8. B -Artemisia Gentileschi

9. B -Mary Cassatt

She was one of the leading artists in the Impressionist Movement of the later part of the 1800's. While many of her Impressionists focused on landscapes and street scenes, she became famous for her portraits.

10. A -Frida Kahlo

11. D -Edmonia Lewis

12. C -Judith Leyster

13. A -Mary Cassatt

14. B -Grandma Moses

Women In History Trivia

15. A -Levina Teerlinc

16. D -Yayoi Kusamen

17. B -Georgia O'Keefe

18. C -Elisabetta Sirani

19. D -Suzanne Valadon

20. A -Berthe Morisot

21. B -Sofonisba Anguissola

22. D -Queenie McKenzie

23. B -Anna Ancher

24. C -Georgia O'Keefe

25. A -Caterina van Hemessen

11

OUTSTANDING ACHIEVEMENTS

Answers for this chapter on page 148

1. She was the first and only to date female Prime Minister of India.

    A. Eva Peron
    B. Valentina Tereshkara
    C. Indira Gandhi
    D. Marie Curie

2. The founder of modern nursing, she was a trailblazing figure in nursing who greatly affected 19th and 20th century policies about proper care in tending to the sick and wounded. She earned the nickname, *'The Lady With The Lamp'* by making rounds during the night checking on soldiers.

    A. Florence Nightingale
    B. Clara Barton
    C. Mary Walker
    D. Rosalind Franklin

3. After an illness while still an infant she was left blind and deaf. Becoming wild and out of control a teacher by the name of Anne Sullivan began a 49-year working relationship with her where she was able to overcome obstacles allowing her to lead a normal life. She overcame the adversity of being blind and deaf to become one

of the 20th century's leading humanitarians as well as founder of the ACLU.

    A. Charlotte Ray   B. Helen Keller

    C. Elizabeth Blackwell   D. Jane Goodall

4. She was the first female pilot to fly across the Atlantic Ocean. While attempting to circumnavigate the globe from the equator she mysteriously disappeared while flying over the Pacific Ocean in 1937. As to her fate, it remains unsolved though there are many unproven theories.

    A. Sally Ride   B. Valentina Tereshkara

    C. Amelia Earhart   D. Ann Morrow Lindbergh

5. She conducted pioneering research on radioactivity. Later working alongside her husband led to the discovery of polonium and radium. When her husband was killed after accidentally stepping in front of a horse-drawn wagon, she took over his teaching post at the Sorbonne becoming the institution's first female professor.

    A. Eleanor Creesy   B. Julia Archibald Holmes

    C. Margaret Chase Smith   D. Marie Curie

6. She was the first woman appointed to the U.S. Supreme Court.

    A. Eva Peron   B. Sandra Day O'Connor

    C. Mary Kies   D. Hillary Clinton

7. She was the most renowned British political leader since Winston Churchill.

    A. Margaret Thatcher   B. Margaret Chase Smith

    C. Rosalind Franklin   D. Elizabeth Blackwell

8. She was an American physicist and astronaut. She became the first American woman in space in the year 1983.

    A. Mary Kies   B. Valentina Tereshkara

    C. Sally Ride   D. Amelia Earhart

9. She is a British primatologist and anthropologist who is considered to be the world's foremost expert on chimpanzees.

    A. Helen Keller   B. Mary Walker

    C. Julia Archibald Holmes   D. Jane Goodall

10. She was the daughter of India's first prime minister and ascended to the position after her father's death in the mid-1960's. As prime minister she led her country into the nuclear age with the detonation of an underground device in 1974.

    A. Indira Gandhi   B. Valentina Tereshkara

    C. Eleanor Creesy   D. Marie Curie

11. At the 1964 Republican Convention, she became the first woman to have her name put in for nomination for the presidency by a major political party.

A. Hillary Clinton   B. Margaret Chase Smith

C. Sandra Day O'Connor   D. Rosalind Franklin

12. She was a First Lady of the United States, a U.S. senator, Secretary of State, and ran twice, unsuccessfully both times, for the presidency.

    A. Eleanor Creesy   B. Julia Archibald Holmes

    C. Hillary Clinton   D. Sandra Day O'Connor

13. When her husband ran for the presidential election in Argentina, she actively campaigned by his side, an unprecedented occurrence in Argentina politics. After he was elected she continued to play an active role working for the betterment of the working class people.

    A. Eva Peron   B. Valentina Tereshkara

    C. Mary Kies   D. Mary Walker

14. She is a retired Russian cosmonaut, engineer, and politician. Having been chosen from more than 400 applicants, she became the first woman to have flown into space.

    A. Marie Curie   B. Julia Archibald Holmes

    C. Indira Gandhi   D. Valentina Tereshkova

15. She was the first woman to receive a medical degree in the U.S.

A. Eleanor Creesy   B. Elizabeth Blackwell

C. Florence Nightingale   D. Mary Walker

16. She was a politician who served as a U.S. Representative and a U.S. senator from Maine, the first woman to serve in both houses of the U.S. Congress and the first woman to represent Maine in either house.

A. Margaret Chase Smith   B. Julia Archibald Holmes

C. Hillary Clinton   D. Rosalind Franklin

17. She was a Polish and naturalized-French physicist and chemist. She remains the most well-known female name in science. She was the first woman to win a Nobel Prize, the first person and only woman to win twice, and the only person to win a Nobel Prize in two different sciences (Physics and Chemistry).

A. Eva Peron   B. Julia Archibald Holmes

C. Marie Curie   D. Indira Gandhi

18. As America's first woman astronaut to travel to space, President Obama posthumously awarded her the Presidential Medal of Freedom, the nation's highest civilian honor in 2013.

A. Eleanor Creesy   B. Sally Ride

C. Mary Kies   D. Jane Goodall

19. In 1960 she left for Gombe National Park in southeastern Africa to begin a study of chimpanzees. She stayed for over two decades producing an amazing set of discoveries about the behaviors and

social interactions of the chimpanzees correcting a number of misunderstandings scientists had of them previous to her work.

    A. Jane Goodall   B. Sally Ride

    C. Helen Keller   D. Charlotte Ray

20. An early 19th century American, she received the first patent granted to a woman by the U.S. Patent & Trademark Office in 1809. She invented a new technique for weaving straw with silk or thread boosting the nation's hat industry.

    A. Eleanor Creesy   B. Julia Archibald Holmes

    C. Margaret Chase Smith   D. Mary Kies

21. She was not the first woman to be issued a pilot's license but she became the first woman to fly across the Atlantic Ocean in 1928 as well as the first person (man or woman) to fly over both the Atlantic and the Pacific.

    A. Sally Ride   B. Amelia Earhart

    C. Anne Morrow Lindbergh   D. Rosalind Franklin

22. She was the longest-serving British Prime Minister of the 20th century and the first woman to have been appointed to the position.

    A. Margaret Chase Smith   B. Margaret Thatcher

    C. Elizabeth Blackwell   D. Elizabeth Windsor

23. In the mid-1850's she opened a clinic in New York for poor

women and children. In 1861 she helped establish the U.S. Sanitary Commission.

    A. Mary Walker   B. Eleanor Creesy

    C. Florence Nightingale   D. Elizabeth Blackwell

24. In 1907 she became the first woman awarded the Order of Merit. The following year she received the Freedom of the City of London, becoming the first woman to receive that honor.

    A. Mary Walker   B. Julia Archibald Holmes

    C. Florence Nightingale   D. Marie Curie

25. American physician and reformer who is believed to be the only woman surgeon formally engaged for field duty during the Civil War.

    A. Mary Walker   B. Florence Nightingale

    C. Clara Barton   D. Rosalind Franklin

26. She was the deciding vote on the controversial Bush vs. Gore case in the year 2000. The ruling effectively ended the recount for the contested 2000 presidential race. Later in hindsight, she admitted perhaps the highest court should not have weighed in based on the circumstances of the election.

    A. Hillary Clinton   B. Sandra Day O'Connor

    C. Margaret Chase Smith   D. Charlotte Ray

27. She was the first African-American female lawyer in the U.S.,

the first female admitted to the District of Columbia Bar, and the first woman admitted to practice before the Supreme Court of the District of Columbia.

    A. Charlotte Ray   B. Sandra Day O'Connor

    C. Margaret Chase Smith   D. Hillary Clinton

28. She was the first woman to climb Pike's Peak.

    A. Elizabeth Blackwell   B. Eleanor Creesy

    C. Rosalind Franklin   D. Julia Archibald Holmes

29. She set many aviation records, wrote best-selling books about her flying experiences, and was instrumental in the formation of the Ninety-Nines, an organization for female pilots. She set the world altitude record for female pilots, and set seven women's speed and distance aviation records. She was the first person to fly solo from Hawaii to the U.S. mainland, among other firsts.

    A. Charlotte Ray   B. Julia Archibald Holmes

    C. Amelia Earhart   D. Sally Ride

30. Working with a fellow scientist they were making progress while studying DNA when they made a startling discovery using X-ray images. The discovery was observed in what was titled 'Photo 51.' One of the scientists who had been working with her removed the photo from her records without her consent or knowledge. 'Photo 51' was the discovery of the Double Helix. It was the proof the scientists needed. The scientists published their findings with no mention of her work or discovery. In 1962 the three scientists accepted the Nobel Peace Prize in Medicine for modeling the structure of the molecule and explaining how the

shape lends itself to replication. Because the Nobel Prize can only be shared by three scientists she was barely mentioned when the others accepted the award. There are many who rightfully believe that much of the credit of this achievement should go to someone who was unrecognized for her work. Who was she?

 A. Eleanor Creesy   B. Marie Curie

 C. Margaret Chase Smith   D. Rosalind Franklin

31. Illegitimate and raised in poverty she was the First Lady of Argentina from 1946 until her death in 1952.

 A. Julia Archibald Holmes   B. Eva Peron

 C. Rosalind Franklin   D. Helen Keller

32. In 2015 her space craft, Vostov 6, was displayed as part of an exhibit at the Science Museum in London called *"Cosmonauts: Birth of the Space Age."*

 A. Valentina Tereshkova   B. Sally Ride

 C. Margaret Chase Smith   D. Elizabeth Blackwell

33. As the Civil War broke out she demanded a spot in the Union Army. Her request for a commission as a medical officer was denied. She volunteered anyway. She earned a spot as an acting assistant surgeon.

 A. Eleanor Creesy   B. Mary Walker

 C. Florence Nightingale   D. Rosalind Franklin

34. Her work on the structures and uses of coal and graphite and her published works on the subject was used in development of the gas masks that helped soldiers during the war.

   A. Marie Curie   B. Julia Archibald Holmes

   C. Margaret Chase Smith   D. Rosalind Franklin

35. She was the female navigator of 'Flying Cloud,' a clipper ship that set the world's sailing record for the fastest passage between New York and San Francisco in 1851.

   A. Mary Kies   B. Julia Archibald Holmes

   C. Rosalind Franklin   D. Eleanor Creesy

Answers - Chapter 11 – Outstanding Achievements

1. C -Indira Gandhi

*When she was first appointed to office in 1966, she gained widespread support for agricultural improvements that led her country to self-sufficiency in food grain production. She was also successful in the Pakistan War which resulted in the creation of Bangladesh. One of her most unpopular policies was government-enforced sterilization as a means of population control. She was assassinated by two of her bodyguards. The bodyguards were both Sikhs. They killed her in retribution for the attack she ordered at the Golden Temple in Amritsar, Punjab. Hundreds of Sikhs were killed in the battle igniting an uprising within the Sikh community. The Golden Temple is the Sikh's holiest temple.

2. A -Florence Nightingale

3. B -Helen Keller

*She was appointed counselor of international relations for the American Foundation of Overseas Blind. She traveled to thirty-five countries on five continents. At age seventy-five she took the hardest journey of her life, covering 40,000 miles in a five month time period across Asia. She brought inspiration and encouragement to millions of people.

4. C -Amelia Earhart

*She became the first woman and the second person (after Charles Lindbergh) to fly solo across the Atlantic Ocean.

5. D -Marie Curie

*When WWI broke out Curie devoted her time to helping the cause. It was due to her that portable x-ray machines were used in the field saving lives of many wounded men. The medical devices were called "Little Curies" after her. In 1995 in recognition of her achievements, her remains and those of her husband were interred in the Pantheon in Paris, the final resting place of France's greatest minds. She was the first of only five women laid to rest there.

6. B -Sandra Day O'Connor

7. A -Margaret Thatcher

8. C -Sally Ride

9. D -Jane Goodall

10. A -Indira Gandhi

11. B -Margaret Chase Smith

12. C -Hillary Clinton

13. A -Eva Peron

*She actively fought for women's suffrage in Argentina which was enacted in 1947 in large part due to her.

14. D -Valentina Tereshkova

*In just under three days she orbited the earth 48 times. When she returned from space she was given the title, 'Hero of the Soviet Union.' She also received the Order of Lenin and the Gold Star Medal. Due to the space mission being Top Secret until it actually occurred, her mother found out about it over the radio while she was orbiting the earth.

15. B -Elizabeth Blackwell

16. A -Margaret Chase Smith

*She became one of the prominent voices of the 20th century politics who supported womens' rights and stood in opposition to Senator McCarthy's crusade against communism. She was honored with the Presidential Medal of Freedom posthumously.

17. C -Marie Curie

18. B -Sally Ride

19. A -Jane Goodall

20. D -Mary Kies

*Prior to 1790 only men could author a patent. The Patent Act of 1790 opened the door for men or women to protect their invention with a patent. Unfortunately, Sybilla Masters received the first patent issued to man or woman in recorded

American history, but it was granted in 1715 so was issued in her husband's name.

21. B -Amelia Earhart

22. B -Margaret Thatcher

23. D -Elizabeth Blackwell

24. C -Florence Nightingale

25. A -Mary Walker

*In 1865 she was awarded the Congressional Medal of Honor – the first and only woman in history to receive the award. In 1917, the terms used to designate eligibility were reappraised and she along with nearly 1,000 recipients were stripped of their medals. As a former Army surgeon who had endured harrowing years along the front she refused to part with her medal. She had worn her Medal of Honor constantly from the day she received it until the day she died -even after it had been revoked. In 1977 President Jimmy Carter restored her medal posthumously.

26. B -Sandra Day O'Connor

27. A -Charlotte Ray

28. D -Julia Archibald Holmes

29. C -Amelia Earhart

30. D -Rosalind Franklin

31. B -Eva Peron

32. A -Valentina Tereshkova

33. B -Mary Walker

*In 1864 she was a prisoner of war for four months and after that time she was exchanged for a Confederate soldier.

34. D -Rosalind Franklin

35. D -Eleanor Creesy

*Her record held until 1989.

12

WOMEN ATHLETES

Answers for this chapter on page 157

1. She is the greatest female track star of all time. She won medals at four different Olympics.

    A. Marlene Hagge   B. Justine Siegel

    C. Jackie Joyner-Kersee   D. Babe Didrikson Zacharias

2. She had the greatest rookie year in the LPGA history.

    A. Martina Navratilova   B. Homerwe Sawa

    C. Lottie Dodd   D. Nancy Lopez

3. She was a gymnast from Romania and was the first female to ever earn a perfect 10 at the Olympics.

    A. Nadia Comaneci   B. Nadine Angerer

    C. Mary Lou Retton   D. Bonnie Blair

4. She was a 19th century English athlete and superstar who was best known as a tennis player. She won Wimbledon five times –

the first when she was only fifteen. She remains the youngest ladies' singles champion.

    A. Lottie Dod   B. Dorothy Campbell

    C. Marlene Hagge   D. Babe Didrikson Zacharias

5. German former professional tennis player, she was ranked World #1 and won 22 Grand Slam singles titles. She became the first and only tennis player (male or female) to achieve the Golden Slam by winning all four Grand Slam singles titles and the Olympic gold medal in the same year.

    A. Martina Navratilova   B. Steffi Graf

    C. Babe Didrikson Zacharias D. Serena Williams

6. Gold medal winning Olympic figure skater, she earned the World Championship title in Sweden and in the U.S. the title of "*America's Sweetheart.*" She received many honors from her career as a figure skater and was inducted into the Olympic Hall of Fame and the Figure Skating Hall of Fame.

    A. Peggy Fleming   B. Lottie Dod

    C. Nadia Comaneci   D. Dorothy Hamill

7. She became the first woman Aboriginal Australian to win an Olympic gold medal.

    A. Nova Peris   B. Marta

    C. Homarwe Sawa   D. Lottie Dod

8. She was the greatest female golfer of the pre-World War II era.

    A. Joyce Wethered   B. Justine Siegel

    C. Toni Stone   D. Babe Didrikson Zacharias

9. She was the first female golfer to score under 300 in a 72-hole tournament, accomplishing this feat at the 1947 U.S. Women's Open.

    A. Marlene Hagge   B. Betty Jameson

    C. Dorothy Campbell   D. Babe Didrikson Zacharias

10. She was the first woman to play baseball in the Negro Leagues with the Kansas City Monarchs. She even got a hit off Satchel Paige when she played for the Indianapolis Clowns.

    A. Toni Stone   B. Marta

    C. Mia Hamm   D. Marlene Hagge

11. This U.S. female soccer player has scored more international goals than any male or female soccer player. She won gold medals in all 3 Olympics she played in, won the AP Female Athlete of the Year Award, and in 2012 was selected FIFA World Player of the Year.

    A. Marta   B. Justine Siegel

    C. Mia Hamm   D. Abby Wambach

12. She won five gold medals at three Olympic games for her speedskating. She won the James E. Sullivan Award which goes to

the top amateur athlete in the country and was named ABC Wide World of Sports Athlete of the Year, and Sports Illustrated Sportsman of the Year.

    A. Mary Lou Retton   B. Bonnie Blair

    C. Babe Didrikson Zacharias   D. Lottie Dod

13. Many call her the top women's tennis player of all time. During her career in tennis she won 18 Grand Slam titles, 31 major women's doubles, and 10 mixed doubles titles. Her 9 Wimbledon wins still holds the record.

    A. Marlene Hagge   B. Martina Navratilova

    C. Serena Williams   D. Steffi Graf

14. She was perhaps the most influential woman athlete of all time. She won gold in both the 80 meter hurdles and javelin throw and a silver in the high jump at the 1932 Summer Olympics. She won the 1946 U.S. Women's Amateur Golf Tournament. She played at three PGA events and became a Hall-Of-Famer at the sport. From 1932 – 1954, six times she was named the Associated Press Female Athlete of the Year.

    A. Joyce Wethered   B. Justine Siegel

    C. Nancy Lopez   D. Babe Didrikson Zacharias

15. According to the 'Guinness Book of Records' she is the most versatile British female athlete of all time. Known best as a tennis player she was also British national golf champion and a member of England's women's national field hockey team, and she won a silver medal at the 1908 Olympics in archery.

A. Marlene Hagge

B. Dorothy Campbell

C. Lottie Dod

D. Babe Didrikson Zacharias

16. She was the first female American to win the all-around gold medal at the Olympics and was the only one to do so for 20 years. She is credited with being a pioneering figure in American women's gymnastics. Winning a gold, 2 silver, and 2 bronze medals at the 1984 Summer Olympics she became one of the most popular athletes in the U.S.

A. Mary Lou Retton

B. Mia Hamm

C. Abby Wambach

D. Nadia Comaneci

17. This Brazilian soccer player has won the FIFA World Player of the Year five times; more than any other female soccer player in history. She is considered as the 2nd best female soccer player of all time.

A. Nadine Angerer

B. Homarwe Sawa

C. Marta

D. Mia Hamm

18. An American former figure skater, she won the only gold medal the U.S. received in the 1968 Olympics.

A. Bonnie Blair

B. Peggy Fleming

C. Jackie Joyner-Kersee

D. Dorothy Hamill

19. She is one of just two female soccer players to be named to the FIFA 100, commemorating the 125 greatest living soccer players.

A. Justine Siegel   B. Abby Wambach

C. Mia Hamm   D. Marta

20. She set the 500 meter speedskating world record (39.10 seconds) and later became the first woman ever to crack the 39.0 second record setting a new world record.

A. Bonnie Blair   B. Dorothy Hamill

C. Abby Wambach   D. Peggy Fleming

Answers – Chapter 12 – Women Athletes

1. C -Jackie Joyner-Kersee

*What many don't know is she was also an outstanding basketball athlete playing seventeen games as a pro basketball player.

2. D -Nancy Lopez

3. A -Nadia Comaneci

*She won five gold Olympic medals. She also earned three silvers and a bronze in Olympic competition. Including the Olympics World Championships, European Championships, and Summer University games she won twenty-one gold medals, seven silvers, and two bronzes.

4. A -Lottie Dod

5. B -Steffi Graf

6. D -Dorothy Hamill

7. A -Nova Peris

8. A -Joyce Wethered

9. B -Betty Jameson

10. A -Toni Stone

11. D -Abby Wambach

12. B -Bonnie Blair

13. B -Martina Navratilova

14. D -Babe Didrikson Zacharias

15. C -Lottie Dod

16. A -Mary Lou Retton

17. C - Marta

18. B - Peggy Fleming

19. C - Mia Hamm

20. A - Bonnie Blair

13

WOMEN IN MUSIC

Answers for this chapter on page 171

1. She was lead singer for the band Jefferson Airplane. She wrote the hits 'White Rabbit' and sang 'Somebody To Love.'

    A. Stevie Nicks   B. Grace Slick

    C. Whitney Houston   D. Linda Ronstadt

2. While she toured with her band in Europe in order to avoid body searches for drugs by customs they hired a private train to travel through Germany, France, and Holland. The luxurious lounge rail car they hired had once belonged to Hitler and even included the attendant who had once served the Führer.

    A. Grace Slick   B. Joni Mitchell

    C. Janis Joplin   D. Stevie Nicks

3. Known for her heavyset figure, she was a member of the 1960's group The Mamas and the Papas. Initially John Phillips, founder of the group, didn't want her to be a part of the band due to her weight – it wasn't 'the look' he wanted, but he couldn't ignore her fantastic voice for long and made her a member of the band.

A. Cass Elliott   B. Janis Joplin

C. Mariah Carey   D. Carly Simon

4. An American singer and songwriter she rose to musical success in the mid-70's as an R&B artist and re-emerged as a pop artist in the late 80's. In the 1990's she recorded renditions of songs previously sung by her famous father, songs such as 'Unforgettable.' Her albums break out single featured a track dubbed over a previous recording of her fathers, as to create a father-daughter duet.

A. Tina Turner   B. Ella Fitzgerald

C. Natalie Cole   D. Brenda Lee

5. She was born into country music royalty and a member of the legendary singing family The Carter Sisters, country music's first self-contained all-female band. She was the second wife of Johnny Cash.

A. Patsy Cline   B. June Cash Carter

C. Loretta Lynn   D. Brenda Lee

6. Multiple Grammy winner, dubbed "Queen of Soul," she is known for her hits, 'Respect,' 'I Say A Little Prayer,' 'You Make Me Feel Like A Woman,' and 'Ain't No Mountain High Enough.'

A. Nina Simone   B. Ella Fitzgerald

C. Ma Rainey   D. Aretha Franklin

7. She not only sang but got into acting by starring with Kevin

Costner in 1992 in the movie 'The Bodyguard.' Each movie she was in she released a hit single from the movie.

    A. Billie Holiday   B. Stevie Nicks

    C. Mariah Carey   D. Whitney Houston

8. She's an American singer and songwriter known for her five-octave range and vocal power. She was the first female artist to accomplish a #1 debut in the U.S. and the only artist since the Beatles to have as many #1 singles and albums.

    A. Mariah Carey   B. Whitney Houston

    C. Joan Baez   D. Linda Ronstadt

9. This legendary singer, songwriter, pianist, arranger, and activist in the Civil Rights Movement sang a mix of jazz, blues, and folk music in the 1950's & 60's. She was one of the most gifted vocalists of her generation.

    A. Joan Baez   B. Nina Simone

    C. Joni Mitchell   D. Ella Fitzgerald

10. She wrote her first #1 hit, 'Will You Love Me Tomorrow' at the age of seventeen. She has become the most celebrated and iconic singer/songwriter of all time.

    A. Carole King   B. Carly Simon

    C. Whitney Houston   D. Mariah Carey

11. Using the music from 'John Brown's Body,' she wrote the lyrics of

'*The Battle Hymn of the Republic*' in 1861, which remains a well-known American patriotic song.

    A. Katherine Lee Bates   B. Ma Rainey

    C. Julia Ward Howe   D. Francesca Caccini

12. She is known as one of the most popular African American entertainers of the 20th century. A woman of great beauty and commanding stage presence she performed in nightclubs, concert halls, movies, and on radio and television.

    A. Lena Horne   B. Whitney Houston

    C. Natalie Cole   D. Aretha Franklin

13. She was best known for her hits '*Crazy*' and '*Walking After Midnight.*'

    A. Billie Holiday   B. June Cash Carter

    C. Loretta Lynn   D. Patsy Cline

14. She was discovered in an amateur talent contest and went on to become the top female jazz singer for decades. This American jazz singer was often referred to as "The First Lady of Songs" and "Queen of Jazz."

    A. Nina Simone   B. Ella Fitzgerald

    C. Cass Elliott   D. Tina Turner

15. By the age of twelve she had starred at The Grand Ole Opry and in Las Vegas. In 1959 she was #1 on the charts with hit '*Sweet*

Nothings.'

    A. Brenda Lee   B. Patsy Cline

    C. June Cash Carter   D. Dolly Parton

16. The 1960's were a turbulent time in American history. She often used her music to express her social and political views. She used her voice for wide spread change. She played a critical role in popularizing Bob Dylan

    A. Joni Mitchell   B. Grace Slick

    C. Joan Baez   D. Linda Ronstadt

17. Songs 'Rhiannon' and 'Landslide' were overnight hits, bringing a lot of attention to the female singer who whirled onstage with flowing outfits and a voice that mesmerized her fans. She is best known for her work with Fleetwood Mac; her solo career, her distinctive voice, and mystical stage persona also make her memorable. With Fleetwood Mac she has produced over 40 top 50 hits and sold over 140 million records making her one of the best selling music acts of all time.

    A. Whitney Houston   B. Stevie Nicks

    C. Janis Joplin   D. Grace Slick

18. She was an American country music star during the late 50's and early 60's. She "crossed over" to pop music and was one of the most influential, successful, and acclaimed vocalists of the 20th century. She died at age thirty in an airplane crash.

    A. Patsy Cline   B. Carole King

    C. Loretta Lynn   D. Dolly Parton

19. She was one of the earliest African American professional blues singers and one of the first generation of blues singers to record. She was billed as "Mother of the Blues."

    A. Tina Turner   B. Lena Horne

    C. Nina Simone   D. Ma Rainey

20. She is not only the definitive female soul singer of the 60's, she's also one of the most influential and important voices in pop history. She fused the gospel music she grew up on with the sensuality of R&B, the innovation of jazz, and the precision of pop.

    A. Whitney Houston   B. Aretha Franklin

    C. Natalie Cole   D. Tina Turner

21. She played at Woodstock in 1969. She was one of the most well-known personalities in Rock & Roll during the 60's. She showed up at the White House for a party hosted by First Daughter Tricia Nixon with intentions of spiking the punch bowl with LSD. Abbie Hoffman had tagged along, but being that he was high on the CIA's Most Wanted List they never made it into the White House.

    A. Stevie Nicks   B. Grace Slick

    C. Joni Mitchell   D. Janis Joplin

22. A top-charting solo female vocalist of the 1960's she sang rockabilly, pop and country music, with 47 U.S. chart hits during the 60's. She is ranked 4th in that decade, surpassed only by Elvis Presley, the Beatles, and Ray Charles. She is best remembered for her hits 'I'm Sorry' and 'Rockin' Around the Christmas Tree.'

A. Brenda Lee   B. Patsy Cline

C. June Cash Carter   D. Dolly Parton

23. She performed and recorded with Benny Goodman Orchestra, went on tour with Dizzy Gillespie and his band, produced recordings with great artists Louis Armstrong, Count Basie, Frank Sinatra, Nat King Cole, and Duke Ellington.

A. Nina Simone   B. Aretha Franklin

C. Ella Fitzgerald   D. Lena Horne

24. Considered one of the best jazz vocalists of all time she was one of the most influential jazz singers with a career that spanned nearly thirty years. She was nicknamed "Lady Day."

A. Natalie Cole   B. Billie Holiday

C. Nina Simone   D. Lena Horne

25. In 1987, she became the first female artist to be inducted into the Rock & Roll Hall of Fame. In 2008 she won her 18th Grammy Award making her one of the most honored artists in Grammy history.

A. Tina Turner   B. Grace Slick

C. Whitney Houston   D. Aretha Franklin

26. A Canadian singer/songwriter, *Rolling Stone Magazine* called her "one of the greatest songwriters ever." Her songs often reflected social and environmental ideals, as well as romance, confusion, disillusionment, and joy. No female artist better typified the

singer/songwriter movement of the 70's better than she did.

   A. Carly Simon   B. Joan Baez

   C. Joni Mitchell   D. Nina Simone

27. She became one of the most distinctive performers in Nashville in the 60's & 70's with her instantly recognizable delivery which made her one of the greatest voices in country music history. She is one of the most awarded musicians of all times and has been inducted into more music halls of fame than any female recording artist, including The Country Music Hall of Fame. She was the first woman to be named the Country Music Association's Entertainer of the Year. She won four Grammy Awards and the Presidential Medal of Freedom.

   A. Loretta Lynn   B. June Cash Carter

   C. Brenda Lee   D. Patsy Cline

28. In 2013 she made music history as the first woman to receive the Gershwin Prize for Popular Song. She received this award at the White House from President Obama.

   A. Carly Simon   B. Carole King

   C. Whitney Houston   D. Joan Baez

29. She wrote the poem 'America the Beautiful,' which became the lyrics to the patriotic ballad.

   A. Julia Ward   B. Francesca Caccini

   C. Cass Elliott   D. Katherine Lee Bates

30. This jazz singer made history in 1958 becoming the first African American woman to win a Grammy Award. She would go on to win thirteen Grammys during her career.

    A. Ella Fitzgerald   B. Aretha Franklin

    C. Natalie Cole   D. Lena Horne

31. In 2009 'Guinness World Records' cited her as the most awarded female act of all time. She was one of the best-selling music artists of all time with 200 million records sold worldwide. She became the first artist ever to have seven consecutive singles hit #1, and her Dolly Parton song, 'I Will Always Love You,' became the biggest hit single in Rock history.

    A. Whitney Houston   B. Carole King

    C. Mariah Carey   D. Aretha Franklin

32. She's an American country music singer-songwriter with multiple gold albums in a career spanning almost sixty years. She is famous for such hits as, 'Don't Come Home A'Drinkin' ' and 'Coal Miner's Daughter.'

    A. June Cash Carter   B. Brenda Lee

    C. Loretta Lynn   D. Patsy Cline

33. She rose to international prominence as a singer with her husband and as a solo performer. One of the world's best-selling artists of all times and according to 'Guinness World Records' she has sold more concert tickets than any other solo performer in history. This Grammy winner is famous for songs, What's Love Got To Do With It' and 'Proud Mary.'

A. Whitney Houston   B. Tina Turner

C. Cass Elliott   D. Natalie Cole

34. She was the first woman to compose opera and the most well-paid musician at the Medici court. She was an Italian composer and singer, one of very few women in 17th century Europe whose compositions were published. She worked at the Medici court in Florence beginning in the early 1600's.

A. Francesca Caccini   B. Mariah Carey

C. Julia Ward Howe   D. Maria Callas

35. She was one of the most successful and widely-known female rock stars of her era. Singer and songwriter, she rose to fame in the late 60's with her powerful blues-inspired vocals. She died of a drug overdose at the age of twenty-seven, but not before making such hits reaching the top of the charts with songs, 'Piece of My Heart,' 'Me and Bobby McGee,' and 'Mercedes Benz.'

A. Tina Turner   B. Aretha Franklin

C. Cass Elliott   D. Janis Joplin

36. She broke new ground when she worked with Artie Shaw and his orchestra becoming one of the first female African American vocalists to work with a white orchestra.

A. Billie Holiday   B. Natalie Cole

C. Ella Fitzgerald   D. Lena Horne

37. This African American jazz and pop singer, actress, and civil

rights activist career spanned over seventy years beginning at the age of sixteen when she joined the chorus at the Cotton Club becoming a nightclub performer. She moved on to Hollywood where she had parts in movies before finding herself blacklisted during the Red Scare during the days of McCarthyism. She was one of the most popular performers of her time. Her trademark song was 'Stormy Weather.'

    A. Brenda Lee   B. Nina Simone

    C. Ma Rainey   D. Lena Horne

38. Not only did she perform at the funeral of Dr. Martin Luther King, Jr., but she also sang the national anthem at the Democratic National Convention. She performed at the 1977 presidential inauguration of Jimmy Carter, the inauguration of Bill Clinton, and at Barack Obama's inauguration.

    A. Natalie Cole   B. Ella Fitzgerald

    C. Aretha Franklin   D. Whitney Houston

39. She was a Greek American soprano and one of the most renowned and influential opera singers of the 20th century. She had a long-lasting affair with Greek shipping magnate, Aristotle Onassis who married former first lady Jacqueline Kennedy.

    A. Nina Simone   B. Maria Callas

    C. Francesca Caccini   D. Ma Rainey

40. She rose to fame in the 70's with a string of hits including, 'Anticipation' and 'You're So Vain.' A Grammy winner, she was one of the biggest singer/songwriters of the '70's. She was the first artist to have won three major awards: Oscar, Grammy, and Golden

Globe for a single hit. She was married to fellow rock star James Taylor.

A. Carly Simon

B. Joni Mitchell

C. Joan Baez

D. Carole King

Answers - Chapter 13 – Women In Music

1. B -Grace Slick

2. D -Stevie Nicks

3. A -(Mama) Cass Elliott

4. C -Natalie Cole

5. B -June Cash Carter

6. D -Aretha Franklin

*She made a cameo appearance in the movie, 'The Blues Brothers' with John Belushi and Dan Aykroyd.

7. D -Whitney Houston

8. A -Mariah Carey

*"Songbird Supreme' was the name given to her by Guinness World Records.

9. B -Nina Simone

10. A -Carole King

*By the end of 1970, this songwriter began to devote herself exclusively to singing her own songs. Some of these songs were: 'So Far Away,' 'I Feel the Earth Move,' and 'You've Got A Friend.'

11. C -Julia Ward Howe

*On her father's side she was descended from Roger Williams and two governors of Rhode Island. Her mother was the great grand niece of Revolutionary War legend Francis Marion, better known as 'The Swamp Fox.'

12. A -Lena Horne

*In 1943 a booking at the Savoy Plaza Hotel not only brought her national coverage, but established her as the highest-paid African American entertainer in the U.S. She became the first African American woman since 1915 to sign a term contract with a film studio.

13. D -Patsy Cline

14. B -Ella Fitzgerald

15. A -Brenda Lee

16. C -Joan Baez

17. B -Stevie Nicks

18. A -Patsy Cline

19. D -Ma Rainey

20. B -Aretha Franklin

*Rolling Stone magazine placed her in the #1 spot on their list of "The Greatest Singers of All Time."

21. B -Grace Slick

22. A -Brenda Lee

23. C -Ella Fitzgerald

*Before her days of fame when only a young girl, she helped her family financially by working as a messenger "running numbers" and acting as a lookout for a brothel.

24. B -Billie Holiday

25. D -Aretha Franklin

26. C -Joni Mitchell

27. A -Loretta Lynn

28. B -Carole King

*She is the most successful female songwriter of the latter half of the 20th century in the U.S. and was the most successful female songwriter on the U.K. Singles charts between 1952 – 2005. She has written or co-written over 400 songs that have been recorded by *more than 1,000 artists.*

29. D -Katharine Lee Bates

30. A -Ella Fitzgerald

31. A -Whitney Houston

In 1991 during the Gulf War, she performed the 'Star Spangled Banner' at Super Bowl XXV. She became the first artist to turn the national anthem into a top 40 hit.

32. C -Loretta Lynn

33. B -Tina Turner

34. A -Francesca Caccini

Her only surviving work, 'La Liberazione di Ruggiero' is widely considered the oldest opera by a woman composer.

35. D -Janis Joplin

36. A -Billie Holiday

37. D -Lena Horne

38. C -Aretha Franklin

39. B -Maria Callas

40. A -Carly Simon

14

ACTRESSES FROM DAYS AGO

Answers for this chapter on page 185

1. She began her career as a child actress with one of her most significant roles, 'Miracle On 34th Street.' She received three Academy Award nominations before the age of twenty-five. As a teenager she performed in 'Rebel Without A Cause' and starred in the musical 'West Side Story.' She drowned in a suspicious death which remains controversial.

    A. Shirley Temple   B. Doris Day

    C. Natalie Wood   D. Olivia de Havilland

2. She sang her way into the hearts of children and adults alike. She starred in such films as 'Mary Poppins' and 'The Sound of Music.' An English actress, singer, and author who lost her singing voice which had ensured her fame when her vocal chords were damaged during an operation.

    A. Judy Garland   B. Julie Andrews

    C. Ginger Rogers   D. Doris Day

3. She was born in Sweden and was one of the most glamorous and popular motion picture stars of the 1920's and 30's. She was well-known for playing roles of strong-willed heroines. She had a mysterious, ethereal screen persona. She became even a bigger star with "talking films," the first of which she played in was 'Anna Christie' in 1930.

    A. Marlene Dietrich   B. Claudette Colbert

    C. Lillian Gish   D. Greta Garbo

4. Before her acting career her name was Norma Jeane. At sixteen years of age she married her neighbor Jim Dougherty, as her foster family was moving out of state and she would have to go back to the orphanage or get married. Her mother had been institutionalized and her father had deserted her. Her first marriage lasted four years. She left him when he gave her the option of being married to him and being a housewife or a star, but was told she couldn't have both.

    A. Rita Hayworth   B. Marilyn Monroe

    C. Deborah Kerr   D. Marlene Dietrich

5. This actress and fashion icon was from Belgium. She was ranked by American Film Institute as the 3rd greatest female screen legend in Golden Age Hollywood. She is one of few actresses to win an Emmy, Tony, Grammy, and Academy Award. She starred in films: 'Gigi,' 'Roman Holiday,' and 'Breakfast At Tiffanys.'

    A. Audrey Hepburn   B. Ingrid Bergman

    C. Natalie Wood   D. Olivia de Havilland

6. She is regarded as one of silent cinema's finest actresses. She has

been called "The First Lady of the Silent Screen."

    A. Clara Bow   B. Lillian Gish

    C. Greta Garbo   D. Mary Pickford

7. The 1960's bombshell was an Italian actress who worked alongside such stars as: Cary Grant, Clark Gable, Frank Sinatra, William Holden, and Paul Newman. She is often listed among the world's all-time most attractive women.

    A. Claudette Colbert   B. Olivia de Havilland

    C. Raquel Welch   D. Sophia Loren

8. She rose to stardom during the days of silent film in the 1920's and was as equally successful in "talkies." She personified the Roaring Twenties and was a leading sex symbol in her day.

    A. Clara Bow   B. Mary Pickford

    C. Carole Lombard   D. Lillian Gish

9. She was a German actress who held both German and American citizenship. She was known for her sultry, sex appeal during the 30's and 40's. She starred in 'Morocco' with Gary Cooper. In 'The Scarlet Empress' she played the role of Russia's Catherine the Great. She starred in several films with John Wayne, Cary Grant, and Jimmy Stewart in the mid-50's. She began a thriving singing career and performed around the world.

    A. Ingrid Bergman   B. Greta Garbo

    C. Marlene Dietrich   D. Rita Hayworth

10. She achieved fame during the 1940's as one of the era's top stars. The press gave her the moniker "The Love Goddess," as she was one of the most glamorous screen idols of the time. She was the top pin-up girl for soldiers during WWII.

    A. Rita Hayworth   B. Deborah Kerr

    C. Vivian Leigh   D. Lauren Bacall

11. "America's Sweetheart" of the silent screen and one of the first film stars. At the height of her career she was one of the richest and most famous women in the U.S. She was an actress, producer, and screenwriter. For a time she was the most powerful woman in Hollywood.

    A. Mae West   B. Lillian Gish

    C. Mary Pickford   D. Clara Bow

12. She often played off-beat roles in the screwball comedies of the 1930's. She was the highest paid star in Hollywood in the late 1930's and was wife #3 of actor Clark Gable. She died in a tragic plane accident a few years after their marriage.

    A. Katharine Hepburn   B. Marlene Dietrich

    C. Doris Day   D. Carole Lombard

13. This British-American actress was one of film's most celebrated stars. She began her career as a child actress in the early 40's and was one of Hollywood's most popular stars in the 50's.

    A. Shirley Temple   B. Elizabeth Taylor

    C. Natalie Wood   D. Judy Garland

14. She was ranked as #10 in 1999 on the American Film Institution's list of greatest female stars of Classic Hollywood Cinema. She will be remembered for her role in 'Whatever Happened To Baby Jane?'

    A. Marlene Dietrich   B. Greta Garbo

    C. Joan Crawford   D. Katharine Hepburn

15. She was the spirited Irish actress who co-starred with John Wayne in 'The Quiet Man.' She was known for playing strong-willed, tempestuous beauties in the 1940's & 50's. She was called "The Queen of Technicolor" because when that film process was first used nothing showed off it's assets better than her vivid red hair, green eyes, and flawless peaches-and-cream complexion.

    A. Jean Arthur   B. Claudette Colbert

    C. Rita Hayworth   D. Maureen O'Hara

16. An actress, singer, and dancer; it's hard to think of her without thinking of her as a twosome with Fred Astaire. Their dancing chemistry was magnificent, but she was also taking on serious roles to show her talent could stand on it's own. She won a Lead Actress Academy Award for her dramatic role in 'Kitty Foyle.' After that film she starred in several other films becoming the highest paid woman in America.

    A. Deborah Kerr   B. Ginger Rogers

    C. Doris Day   D. Julie Andrews

17. An actress whose career spanned seven decades, she is well-known for her lighthearted bawdy double entendres. She made her first stage appearance at the age of five at a church social.

A. Mae West   B. Jean Arthur

C. Greta Garbo   D. Bette Davis

18. This British actress is best known for her role as Scarlet in 'Gone With The Wind.'

   A. Audrey Hepburn   B. Deborah Kerr

   C. Vivien Leigh   D. Olivia de Havilland

19. This Swedish actress won three Academy Awards, two Emmys, four Golden Globes, a BAFTA Award, and a Tony for Best Actress. She is most remembered for her role in 'Casablanca.' She starred along with Cary Grant in Alfred Hitchcock's thriller 'Notorious' and was equally mesmerizing in her role in 'For Whom The Bell Tolls' about the Spanish Civil War.

   A. Rita Hayworth   B. Ingrid Bergman

   C. Carole Lombard   D. Lauren Bacall

20. She sang and tap danced and starred in movies reaching worldwide fame like no other child star has ever been able to achieve. Her staircase tap dance with African-American Bill (Bojangles) Robinson is her most remembered moment on film even today.

   A. Judy Garland   B. Natalie Wood

   C. Shirley Temple   D. Ginger Rogers

21. This American actress was known for her distinctive voice and

sultry looks. She was married to Humphrey Bogart.

    A. Lauren Bacall   B. Katharine Hepburn

    C. Greta Garbo   D. Elizabeth Taylor

22. The daughter of vaudeville professionals, she started her career as a child. Her first public performance was when she was just two. She signed a movie contract with MGM at age thirteen. She co-starred with friend Mickey Rooney in 'Love Finds Andy Hardy,' and they co-starred in several more Andy Hardy films. She co-starred with Gene Kelly in a musical, but she will always be remembered for her role as Dorothy in 'The Wizard of Oz' which showcased her singing talents as well as her acting abilities.

    A. Shirley Temple   B. Doris Day

    C. Natalie Wood   D. Judy Garland

23. While still a teenager she began singing on radio and would go on to work as a vocalist with bands. One of her popular recordings was 'Sentimental Journey.' With her wholesome looks she became a leading Hollywood star in the 1950's & 60's making several musicals. She came to epitomize the ideal American woman of the 50's and even starred in some sex comedies making her a leading box-office attraction. You may remember her from films, 'Calamity Jane,' 'Pillow Talk,' 'Please Don't Eat The Daisies,' and the Hitchcock movie 'The Man Who Knew Too Much' where she sang the song, 'Que Sera Sera.'

    A. Doris Day   B. Julie Andrews

    C. Judy Garland   D. Claudette Colbert

24. This American actress was a major film star of the 1930's and

40's. She had feature roles in three Frank Capra films: 'Mr. Deeds Goes To Town,' 'You Can't Take It With You,' and 'Mr. Smith Goes To Washington.'

    A. Elizabeth Taylor   B. Carole Lombard

    C. Deborah Kerr   D. Jean Arthur

25. A British actress she played in several Shakespeare's plays, the musical 'Cabaret,' and played the part of M in James Bond movies. It was her serious roles such as playing Queen Victoria and Queen Elizabeth I that show how highly skilled she is in her acting career.

    A. Elizabeth Taylor   B. Judi Dench

    C. Rita Hayworth   D. Vivien Leigh

26. She is regarded as one of the greatest actresses in history. She was in 'Whatever Happened to Baby Jane?' which revitalized her career. She became the first woman to receive the American Film Institute Life Achievement Award. She was recognized by her heavy-cast eyes and distinctive mannerisms.

    A. Katharine Hepburn   B. Ingrid Bergman

    C. Bette Davis   D. Greta Garbo

27. By the age of six she won an honorary Academy Award and earned $3 million before reaching puberty, and in the 1930's no less.

    A. Shirley Temple   B. Doris Day

    C. Natalie Wood   D. Judy Garland

28. She has won four Academy Awards for Best Actress, more than any other actress in the history of the Academy Awards. She was a leading lady in Hollywood for more than sixty years. To name just a few films she was known for was: 'The African Queen,' 'Guess Who's Coming To Dinner,' 'The Lion In Winter,' and 'On Golden Pond.'

    A. Elizabeth Taylor   B. Maureen O'Hara

    C. Ingrid Bergman   D. Katharine Hepburn

29. Not only a famous actress, but she was for a time married to baseball great Joe DiMaggio. Some of her movies were: 'Gentlemen Prefer Blondes,' 'Some Like It Hot,' and 'How To Marry A Millionaire.'

    A. Jean Arthur   B. Marilyn Monroe

    C. Marlene Dietrich   D. Doris Day

30. Playing the part of Melanie in 'Gone With The Wind' made this British-American beauty a star. She was the sister of Joan Fontaine, also an actress. She was often paired with Errol Flynn playing Maid Marion to his Robin Hood in one film in which they both starred. One of her most notable roles was in 'Hush, Hush Sweet Charlotte.' During WWII she toured military hospitals showing her support to the soldiers.

    A. Vivian Leigh   B. Carole Lombard

    C. Lauren Bacall   D. Olivia de Havilland

31. This ringleted ingenue with an expression of sweet sincerity and invincible innocence in the early 1900's was paid $350,000 for some of her films. Most remember her married to Douglas Fairbanks living at Pickfair, the lavish estate they built. She was a co-founder of United Artists.

| A. Mary Pickford | B. Shirley Temple |
| C. Lillian Gish | D. Clara Bow |

32. She is one of the great British actresses to have made a significant contribution to American films. 'From Here To Eternity' with co-star Burt Lancaster they made love on the beach as waves crashed against them which remains one of Hollywood's steamiest in film history. She was equally sensational in 'The King and I' and in 'Heaven Knows, Mr. Allison.'

| A. Katharine Hepburn | B. Claudette Colbert |
| C. Deborah Kerr | D. Lauren Bacall |

33. Her acting career spanned seventy-five years from 1912 in silent film to "talkies" through 1987.

| A. Clara Bow | B. Lillian Gish |
| C. Greta Garbo | D. Mary Pickford |

34. She was a Paris-born American stage and film actress. She preferred the stage, but did so well in Hollywood she remained there. She was in 'The Hole In The Wall' with Edward G. Robinson. Once she played "the wickedest woman in history," wife of Nero in 'The Sign of the Cross,' her career was secure.

| A. Audrey Hepburn | B. Mae West |
| C. Claudette Colbert | D. Olivia de Havilland |

35. As a child actress, she was Hollywood's number one box office

draw from 1935 – 1938, beating even Clark Gable and Bing Crosby. As an adult she served as a U.S. ambassador and Chief of Protocol serving under four presidents.

A. Shirley Temple

B. Doris Day

C. Natalie Wood

D. Judy Garland

Answers - Chapter 14 — Actresses From Days Ago

1. C - Natalie Wood

2. B - Julie Andrews

3. D - Greta Garbo

4. B - Marilyn Monroe

5. A - Audrey Hepburn

*During much of WWII she studied in the Netherlands. After the Nazis invaded the country she and her mother struggled to survive. She reportedly helped the resistance movement by delivering messages. After the war she studied ballet in Amsterdam and London, making her stage debut in London. At the age of twenty-two she went to New York to star in a production on Broadway...and the rest is history.

6. B - Lillian Gish

7. D - Sophia Loren

*She grew up in poverty in what is described as "perhaps the most squalid city in Italy." Illegitimate, she lived with her mother and other relatives at the home of her grandparents where she shared a bedroom with eight people. After WWII life became even more difficult. She was quoted in an interview about living during the famine being so great that her mother occasionally had to siphon off a cup of water from the car radiator to ration between her two daughters.

8. A - Clara Bow

9. C - Marlene Dietrich

*Adolf Hitler ordered her to return to Germany to make films, which she refused to do. Douglas Fairbanks, Jr., one of her lovers said she confessed to him of her plot to assassinate Hitler. The opportunity never arose.

10. A - Rita Hayworth

11. C - Mary Pickford

12. D -Carole Lombard

13. B -Elizabeth Taylor

*She started dancing at the age of three and gave a recital for Princess Margaret and Elizabeth who would later become the queen. She made her stage debut at the age of ten. She became a huge star at the age of twelve with 'National Velvet.' As a teenager she dated millionaire Howard Hughes and her first marriage was with hotel heir, Nicky Hilton. She married eight times in all – twice to Richard Burton.

14. C -Joan Crawford

*Before her days in Hollywood she starred in at least two porn films and was blackmailed by her brother who threatened to leak them. She had a rivalry with Bette Davis and her reputation will forever be blemished from the book her adopted daughter wrote about her abusive mother.

15. D -Maureen O'Hara

16. B -Ginger Rogers

17. A -Mae West

18. C -Vivien Leigh

19. B -Ingrid Bergman

20. C -Shirley Temple (Black)

21. A -Lauren Bacall

22. D -Judy Garland

23. A -Doris Day

24. D -Jean Arthur

25. B -Judi Dench

*At age eighty she got a tattoo. It's inside her wrist and says, "Carpe diem."

26. C -Bette Davis

27. A -Shirley Temple

Women In History Trivia

28. D -Katharine Hepburn

29. B -Marilyn Monroe

30. D -Olivia de Havilland

31. A -Mary Pickford

32. C -Deborah Kerr

33. B -Lillian Gish

34. C -Claudette Colbert

35. A -Shirley Temple (Black)

*Her first diplomatic post was as a U.S. delegate to the United Nations by President Nixon, ambassador to Ghana appointed by President Ford, ambassador to Czechoslovakia appointed by President George H.W. Bush, first female U.S. Chief of Protocol at the State Department under President Ford, and she worked for the Department of State as a foreign-affairs officer-expert under President Reagan.

15

WOMEN OF MODERN AMERICAN HISTORY

1900's - 2000's

Answers for this chapter on page 198

1. An American socialite and philanthropist she is the most well-known survivor of the Titanic. She is best remembered for exhorting the crew in Lifeboat #6 to return to the debris field where the Titanic sank to look for survivors.

    A. Geraldine Lucas   B. Violet Jessup

    C. Molly Brown   D. Clara Barton

2. She was a much-admired actress and Alfred Hitchcock's favorite leading lady, but she gave it all up to marry a prince and become princess of Monaco.

    A. Rosie the Riveter   B. Grace Kelly

    C. Madeline Astor   D. Clara Barton

3. She was deemed "the most dangerous Allied Spy" during WWII.

A. Virginia Hall   B. Amelia Earhart

C. Ida Straus   D. Elsie Ott

4. There were two female crew members killed in the Space Shuttle 'Challenger' disaster in 1986. Who were they?

A. Sally Ride   B. Christa McAuliffe

C. Rachel Carson   D. Judith Resnik

5. She was the granddaughter of a president, spent part of her youth in the White House, married a Russian prince, and became a princess who was forced to flee Russia with her jewels sewn in her clothing during the Bolshevik Revolution in 1917.

A. Mary Custis Lee   B. Julia Grant Cantacuzene

C. Reba Whittle   D. Adelicia Acklen

6. This female American physicist worked on the Manhattan Project at Los Alamos.

A. Geraldine Lucas   B. Madam C.J. Walker

C. Vicki Van Meter   D. Elizabeth "Diz" Riddle Graves

7. Her design for the Vietnam Veterans Memorial which she submitted at the age of 21, an impressive fact on it's own, was the design chosen for the monument.

A. Maya Lin   B. Violet Jessup

C. Anne Morrow Lindbergh   D. Katharine Wright

8. Homesteaders weren't just men. In 1912, a 47 year-old divorcee, she homesteaded 160 acres at the base of the Grand Tetons and became the second woman to climb it's peak.

    A. Molly Brown   B. Geraldine Lucas

    C. Rachel Carson   D. Reba Whittle

9. A German-Jewish American and co-owner of Macy's department store, his wife refused to leave the 'Titanic' without her husband. Husband and wife were last seen on deck holding hands before a large wave washed them out to sea. His body was recovered, her body was not.

    A. Madeline Astor   B. Violet Jessup

    C. Ida Straus   D. Molly Brown

10. In 1983 she became the first American woman in space.

    A. Christie McAuliffe   B. Sally Ride

    C. Katharine Wright   D. Judith Resnik

11. She was the most famous flapper during the Roaring Twenties and The Jazz Age.

    A. Ziegfeld Follies   B. Elsie Ott

    C. Norma McCorvey   D. Clara Bow

12. She is considered the first female self-made millionaire in the U.S. after founding a company (named after her) that developed and marketed beauty products for black women.

A. Madeline Astor　　　　　　B. Madam C.J. Walker

　　C. Rose Mitchtom　　　　　　D. Julia Grant Cantacuzene

13. She was perhaps the most famous member of the Woman's Christian Temperance Union (WCTU) as she made a name for herself when she went into saloons with a hatchet and demolished barrooms.

　　A. Carry A. Nation　　　　　　B. Molly Brown

　　C. Jane Addams　　　　　　　D. Elizabeth "Diz" Riddle Graves

14. They were a series of elaborate theatrical productions on Broadway in New York City from 1907 – 1931 that were inspired by the Parisian Folies Bergère. The productions featured beautiful chorus girls who sang and danced who were known as what?

　　A. Grace Kelly　　　　　　　B. Marina Oswald

　　C. Ziegfeld Follies　　　　　　D. Violet Jessup

15. She became a symbol for women's role in the defense industry, an icon of WWII.

　　A. Eleanor Roosevelt　　　　　B. Amelia Earhart

　　C. Ethel Rosenberg　　　　　　D. Rosie the Riveter

16. Forty-seven year old American businessman and descendant of the first multi-millionaire in the U.S., the richest person aboard the Titanic didn't survive. His second wife, nineteen years of age and five months pregnant at the time did survive. Who was she?

A. Julia Grant Cantacuzene   B. Ida Straus

C. Madeline Astor   D. Rose Mitchtom

17. *Roe vs. Wade*, the legal case from 1973 in which the Supreme Court decision established a woman's legal right to an abortion. "Jane Roe," the fictitious name used in order to protect the identity of the plaintiff is now known to be who?

A. Norma McCorvey   B. Reba Whittle

C. Elizabeth "Ann" Swift   D. Virginia Hall

18. She was first lady of Arkansas and also first lady of the nation, wife of the president. She was a New York senator, Secretary of State, and ran twice, both times unsuccessfully, for the presidency of the United States.

A. Melania Trump   B. Eleanor Roosevelt

C. Hillary Clinton   D. Geraldine Lucas

19. She along with her husband, American citizens were executed for treason and conspiracy to commit espionage, relating to passing information about the atomic bomb to the Soviet Union.

A. Molly Brown   B. Ida Straus

C. Ethel Rosenberg   D. Marina Oswald

20. A nurse, she was the only U.S. female soldier to be imprisoned as a POW during WWII in the European theater of war.

A. Reba Whittle   B. Rachel Carson

C. Jane Addams   D. Virginia Hall

21. In 1979, sixty-six American embassy workers in Tehran, Iran were taken hostage. Of the fifty-two who were held captive until 1981 two of the hostages were women. Do you know who these women were?

    A. Elsie Ott   B. Vicki Van Meter

    C. Kathryn Koob   D. Elizabeth "Ann" Swift

22. There probably isn't a child alive that hasn't had a teddy bear at one time. The *Washington Post* had put a political cartoon in the paper of how President "Teddy" Roosevelt while hunting wouldn't shoot an old black bear who had been injured by the guide's dogs and then tied to a tree so the president could shoot a bear. The president refused to shoot the bear feeling it would be unsportsmanlike behavior. After the political cartoon came out this woman and her husband who were store owners made the first stuffed bear naming it after the president. Who was she?

    A. Rose Mitchtom   B. Madam C.J. Walker

    C. Clara Bow   D. Geraldine Lucas

23. Which first lady suggested to the president that he destroy the Watergate tapes while they were still private property?

    A. Eleanor Roosevelt   B. Pat Nixon

    C. Nancy Reagan   D. Melania Trump

24. One of the survivors of the 'Titanic,' an ocean liner stewardess and nurse, also survived the 'Brittanic,' sister ship to the 'Titanic.' She was also aboard the 'Olympic' when it collided with another ship. Who was this woman who survived these three disasters at sea?

    A. Molly Brown   B. Ida Straus

    C. Madeline Astor   D. Violet Jessup

25. Melania Trump made history when she became the second First Lady who was not born in America. Who was the 1st foreign born First Lady?

    A. Clara Bow   B. Dolley Madison

    C. Elizabeth Monroe   D. Louisa Adams

26. The Barbie doll was invented in 1959 by a woman who was co-founder of Mattel.

    A. Violet Jessup   B. Ruth Handler

    C. Grace Kelly   D. Judith Resnik

27. The most notorious crime of the 1930's was the kidnapping of the son of a famous man and his wife which made world news in 1932. The mother of the child was wife of a famous aviator and she was an author. Who was the mother of the kidnapped toddler?

    A. Amelia Earhart   B. Katharine Wright

    C. Grace Kelly   D. Anne Morrow Lindbergh

28. A pioneer in air evacuation of military casualties in "Air

Ambulances," a trained nurse and in the Army Air Corps, she was assigned to the first evacuation flight and would become the first woman to receive the U.S. Air Medal.

    A. Christie McAuliffe   B. Clara Barton

    C. Elsie Ott   D. Elizabeth "Diz"Riddle Graves

29. Her two famous brothers never attended college, but their sister did. After graduating she taught at a local high school but also helped at her brothers' bicycle shop. She nursed one brother back to health after he was injured in a crash while flying. She traveled with her brothers to Europe to help sell their flying machine to the French. Who was she?

    A. Amelia Earhart   B. Sally Ride

    C. Katharine Wright   D. Judith Resnik

30. Her book, 'Silent Spring' raised awareness of environmental concerns and led to the reversal of national policies on pesticides. She inspired the movement that led to the creation of the Environmental Protection Agency for which she received the President's Medal of Freedom.

    A. Rachel Carson   B. Norma McCorvey

    C. Geraldine Lucas   D. Maya Lin

31. She was the wife of the man who was accused of assassinating President Kennedy. Over half of all Americans today believe that there is more to this story than a lone gunman shooting and killing the president. It remains one of the largest American conspiracy theories.

A. Christie McAuliffe   B. Marina Oswald

C. Ida Straus   D. Judith Resnik

32. She was the first female aviator to fly solo across the Atlantic Ocean and might have been the first to fly around the world had her plane not vanished. The mystery of what happened to the famous aviator remains unsolved.

   A. Amelia Earhart   B. Vicki Van Meter

   C. Katharine Wright   D. Judith Resnik

33. She co-founded Hull House in Chicago, Illinois; the first settlement house in the U.S., which opened it's doors to recently arrived European immigrants. She was the first woman to receive the Nobel Peace Prize in 1931 for her work on social and world issues.

   A. Elizabeth "Diz" Riddle Graves   B. Elsie Ott

   C. Madam C.J. Walker   D. Jane Addams

34. She became the youngest pilot, at age twelve, to fly across the Atlantic Ocean.

   A. Christie McAuliffe   B. Vicki Van Meter

   C. Amelia Earhart   D. Sally Ride

35. At the urging of what First Lady did General George Marshall support the idea of introducing a woman's service branch in the Army?

Women In History Trivia

A. Bess Truman

B. Eleanor Roosevelt

C. Sarah Jackson

D. Julia Tyler

Answers - Chapter 15 – Women of Modern American History

1. C - Molly Brown

*Despite the way the media and Hollywood portrayed her, she was not ostracized by society nor rejected by her family. The family tried for a time to correct Hollywood's image of her but eventually withdrew from the public refusing to speak to reporters. Who was the "real" Unsinkable Molly Brown? After the Titanic struck the iceberg she helped load others into lifeboats until she too was forced aboard Lifeboat #6. She helped command a lifeboat using her fluency in several languages to assist survivors. She and the other women in the lifeboat worked to row and keep the spirits of the others up. Once aboard the Carpathia she assisted the survivors. By the time they reached New York she had helped establish the Survivors' Committee, been elected as chair, and raised almost $10,000 for destitute survivors. She remained on the Carpathia until all the survivors were met by family or friends or had the medical assistance they needed. She would later (in 1912) present Captain Rostron of the Carpathia a silver cup for his heroism, as well as medals for every member of the crew of the Carpathia. She aided in the erection of the Titanic Memorial in Washington, D.C.

2. B - Grace Kelly

3. A - Virginia Hall

*She had wanted to join the U.S. Foreign Service which led her to an embassy post in Turkey. She accidentally shot her leg off in a hunting accident and forever after walked with a limp with a wooden leg. She went to work during WWII in France as an ambulance driver until Germany invaded France. The U.S. Embassy at that time asked her to provide intelligence and she was recruited as a spy posing as working for the 'New York Post.' She was the first female S.O.E. Operative sent into France. She helped smuggle out information and prisoners while at the same time smuggling in agents and supplies. When the situation grew too dangerous she escaped, limping across the treacherous Pyrenees Mountains on foot in the dead of winter (remember she shot her foot off and had a wooden leg; not only that; crossing the Pyrenees, especially in the dead of winter was quite a feat in itself). But, that isn't the end of her story. Once back in Britain she joined the O.S.S. (American version of S.O.E. which later became the CIA). She was sent back to France disguised as an old woman where she was a radio operator monitoring German intelligence. She organized drops of supplies which enabled fighters to sabotage rail lines, tunnels, and bridges.

4. B & D-Christie McAuliffe & Judith Resnik

5. B -(Princess) Julia Grant Cantacuzene

*Granddaughter of General and President Ulysses S. Grant, daughter of his son Fred Grant

6. D -Elizabeth "Diz" Riddle Graves

7. A -Maya Lin

8. B -Geraldine Lucas

9. C -Ida Straus

10. B -Sally Ride

11. D -Clara Bow

12. B -Madam C.J. Walker

13. A -Carry A. Nation

*Some said her actions were that of a deranged person. The famous psychologist Karl Menninger didn't believe that to be the case. She did come with some baggage though. Her father was a wealthy plantation owner, but it was mainly his slaves who raised her; not even being allowed to eat at the dinner table with her parents. Her mother suffered from mental issues thinking she was a lady-in-waiting to the Queen of England and eventually believed that she was the queen. Carry married a man not realizing he was a severe alcoholic and it is here where she most likely became so strongly convicted against alcoholic. They had a daughter who suffered emotional difficulties that Carry believed to be brought on by her husband's drinking. Friends who knew her described her as kind, loving, and charitable.

14. C -Ziegfeld Follies

15. D -Rosie the Riveter

16. C -Madeline Astor

17. A -Norma McCorvey

*She later became an anti-abortion activist.

18. C -Hillary Clinton

19. C -Ethel Rosenberg

20. A -Reba Whittle

21. C & D -Kathryn Koob & Elizabeth "Ann" Swift

*They spent 444 days as hostages. It was the first time an entire embassy had been held hostage outside of a war situation.

22. A -Rose Michtom

*The year after the first teddy bear was made the Ideal Toy Company was born and soon became a multi-million dollar business. Sixty years later their son was running the business and contacted Kermit Roosevelt, grandson of the president, and asked if his children would pose with one of the original bears. They did and that bear is now displayed in the Smithsonian.

23. B -Pat Nixon

24. D -Violet Jessup

25. D -Louisa Adams

*The 1st First Lady who was foreign born was Louisa Adams wife to the 6th president John Quincy Adams.

26. B -Ruth Handler

*Barbie was first introduced to the world at the American Toy Fair in New York City. The Ken doll came out two years later. Barbie and Ken were named after the children of Ruth Handler. Barbie is the world's most popular doll and an American icon. Today, more than a billion Barbie dolls have been sold in 150 countries.

27. D -Anne Morrow Lindbergh

28. C -Elsie Ott

29. C -Katharine Wright

*She was the sister of Orville and Wilbur Wright who invented, built, and flew the world's first successful airplane in 1903.

30. A -Rachel Carson

31. B -Marina Oswald

32. A -Amelia Earhart

33. D -Jane Addams

34. B -Vicki Van Meter

35. B -Eleanor Roosevelt